John Lash was born in 1948 and spent his youth in Texas. He has studied and practised Tai Chi and Taoist thought for many years. During his personal spiritual journey, he has lived and studied with Sikhs, Hindus and Jewish people, and on his travels he has visited, among others, the holy shrines of Islam, Christianity, Jainism and Buddhism. He is a teacher of Tai Chi and operates the Harmonious Dragon Tai Chi School in Berne, Switzerland.

The Spirit of Tai Chi

John Lash

vega

ISBN 1-84333-202-7

A catalogue record for this book is available
from the British Library

Published in 2002 by

Vega

64 Brewery Road

London, N7 9NT

A member of **Chrysalis** Books plc
Visit our website at www.chrysalisbooks.co.uk

Printed in Great Britain
by CPD, Wales

Contents

Preface

Many times, as a Tai Chi teacher, I have received telephone calls from people wanting to know what Tai Chi is. The same question arises when I do a Tai Chi demonstration to a new class. The problem is that Tai Chi is an experience, a way of life, and words cannot express the truth of it. One can talk about Tai Chi, but one cannot say what it is. However, one can say what it is not.

From the beginning, the student should understand that Tai Chi is not something one can study, like jazz dancing, ballet, piano-playing, or French cooking. A person can go to a French cookery class on Wednesday from 7 pm to 8 pm and when the class is over the student need not think about French cooking again until 7 pm on the following Wednesday. On such courses, the student is learning about one of the innumerable aspects of life. The oriental disciplines, on the other hand, are totalities, a way of approaching all of life and thus must be practised every second of every day. Karate, for instance, is not just a system of moves for self-defence. The movements that one learns from 7 pm to 8 pm are not enough. Karate also requires the development of a state of mind and spirit that reflects the world as it is seen through the discipline's philosophy. It is the same with all oriental disciplines: Zen archery, flower arrangement, calligraphic painting, yoga, or Tai Chi.

Jazz dancing teaches the student about dancing. Tai Chi teaches the student about life. The student must carry the Tai Chi with him every second. During the exercises, the mind, soul, breath, balance, co-ordination, and various parts of the body are combined to work simultaneously and spontaneously during each movement. In other words, the total person is acting totally here and now. When the class is over, the Tai Chi does not stop. As the student reaches for the door handle to leave the classroom, the same process of Oneness should be occurring that was present when the student was doing the Tai Chi movements. When the student has this ability, then all life becomes Tai Chi. There should be the same state of Oneness, whether one is making a Tai Chi movement, making love, cutting a tomato, or walking down a street.

All of the above is simply to demonstrate that to understand an oriental discipline, one must understand the ideas and world view upon which the discipline rests. That is why the oriental disciplines can never be merely hobbies or pastimes. One of the most difficult tasks of the Tai Chi teacher is to make sure that Western students understand this.

In the Western world, our search for personal independence and individuality has taken almost all the meaning out of life. Those aspects of our societies that have traditionally given our lives meaning – religion, family, patriotism, etc. – have been steadily weakened in our search to be free. We have become people without roots, seeking gratification of our personal desires with no concept of responsibility to others or to the rest of the universe. We have rejected meaning in our lives because meaning implies responsibility. We want amusement and entertainment, not duties and responsibilities. We seek to turn the oriental disciplines into hobbies and sports and thus we lose the essence of these arts. Yoga without god is no longer yoga, but Indian gymnastics. Tai Chi without Tao (Oneness) is no longer Tai Chi, but Chinese exercise.

To turn the oriental disciplines into hobbies divorced from their traditional meaning can make the study of these disciplines more harmful than beneficial. In the research section of *The Texas Aggie* (Vol. 68), published by Texas A & M University, the findings of Michael Trulson from his enquiry into the oriental disciplines are described. While his enquiry dealt specifically with karate, his findings are true for all of these disciplines. I quote from the article:

> Some traditional martial arts training can be effective in reducing juvenile delinquency...but 'modernized' forms of martial arts greatly increase aggressive tendencies among delinquents.

> Dr. Michael Trulson found that delinquents who were taught the traditional philosophy and psychology of martial arts as well as the physical aspects showed less aggressiveness and lower anxiety, more self-esteem and increased awareness of social values even a year after training...

> Results, published by the journal Human-Relations, clearly showed lower juvenile delinquent tendencies among those taught the philosophical aspects of

martial arts and increases in delinquent behaviour by those taught only the skills of punching and kicking...

an estimated 10 million Americans have taken some form of martial arts lessons and another half-million sign up each year...

The majority of these clubs and schools teach only fighting and self-defence techniques and our findings suggest that this type of training greatly enhances negative personality traits.

The Western tendency to strip oriental disciplines of their meaning is the reason for writing this book. It will be an attempt to explain the traditional philosophy and psychology of Tai Chi. It will not try to explain what Tai Chi is but, rather, to describe where the student is heading and how the Tai Chi movements help him or her to arrive there. There are several works on Tai Chi presently available. Most usually they present sections about Yin and Yang Chi, health, a little history, and the author's style of Tai Chi. These books exist mainly for the purpose of advertisement. There are no books that explain the 'why' of Tai Chi and the transformation the student must make in order to develop as a Tai Chi person. I hope my volume will help to fill this gap.

The contents of this book are a result of my own years of experience of teaching and practising Tai Chi. For their invaluable help on my journey towards the Tao, I would like to thank Betty Unterberger, my spiritual guide, who started me on the path; Master Charles Lin, who showed me the beauty of Tai Chi; Ted Sturm of the University of New Mexico, who so patiently guided me through Taoist philosophy; Larry Farmer, a good friend who remained with me through all the twists and turns of my journey; my wife and children, who taught me the limitless depths of love; my Tai Chi students whose continual questioning forced me to look ever deeper into the meaning of Tai Chi. May this book help them in their own journey to the Tao.

1
The Tao

According to ancient Chinese thought, the universe is a vast Oneness, a great Unity. This perception is not uncommon among 'primitive' peoples. Such peoples live in a closeness to nature that demands harmony between humanity and the universe as the price of survival. The Chinese realised that everything is dependent upon everything else, and that harmony is the basic principle of existence. The tree needs the rain in order to produce acorns. The wild pig needs the acorns for food. The droppings of the wild pig fertilise the soil. As a result, the surrounding vegetation flourishes, which enables the soil to retain water for the tree. Hence there is no dependence or independence in the universe, but only interdependence. The universe is a vast tapestry in which every star, every creature, every rock, and every drop of water is an essential thread helping to hold all the other threads together. This Oneness of all that exists is called 'Tao'.

This tapestry that is the Tao has a peculiar characteristic. Its threads are always moving, adjusting, and changing their relationships. Change is the only constant in the Tao. But in all this ceaseless change, the harmony of the threads is maintained. The Tao, like a tapestry, cannot be separated into its individual threads, otherwise the Oneness would be lost, the harmony destroyed. Thus it is natural that the Chinese were concerned with maintaining their harmony with the unceasing flow of change in the Tao. Loss of harmony could only result in conflict, separation, and disaster.

With the human body, it is the same. Like the Tao, the body is also a totality, a unity. As long as all the parts co-operate with one another, the body will be healthy. If, however, one part of the body goes its own separate way in competition and conflict with the other parts, then the whole will be destroyed. Cancer, for instance, is just such a process of separation, conflict, and competition.

The Tao cannot be divided into you–me, them–us, nature–humanity, good–evil, capitalist–communist, Jewish–Christian, etc. Separation is disease. There is only the Tao, the Oneness, and humans must live in harmony and co-operation with this Oneness. Realising the need for harmony, the Chinese sought to discover which principles the Tao followed. They observed that the movement of the Tao is continuous and cyclical. Night follows day, death follows life, winter follows summer, all in a never-ending cycle. Hence, the Chinese saw the Tao as a circle within which all things exist and move.

In the process of moving, the Tao divides into Yin and Yang Chi, or vital energy. These two energies flow through the universe like two mighty rivers. The Yin Chi is 'feminine', non-aggressive, yielding, and receptive. The Yang Chi is 'masculine', strong, aggressive, and outgoing. The Yin and Yang flow together to form objects. Everything is composed of a combination of Yin and Yang Chi. A certain combination produces a tree, a different combination produces a human being, and so forth. When the two Chis separate, the object disappears back into the Void, or Wu Chi, the original emptiness of the Tao.

In other words, the Tao is like a vast ocean composed of the waters of Chi. The Chi currents flow through this ocean causing waves, eddies, whirlpools, etc. The Tao is continuously-flowing never-ending movement. And like the ocean it is a system in which all the parts are harmonised and interdependent. The individual human is like a fish in this great ocean. We can struggle against the flow of the Tao, be in conflict with the other parts (other human beings, nature, etc.), or we can harmonise ourselves with the flow of the whole.

With human beings, some people are predominantly Yin (non-aggressive, etc.) while others are predominantly Yang (aggressive, competitive, etc.). In fact, everything divides into Yin and Yang. The Western world is Yang. In the Western world, we seek the answers to life with our rational minds, using science and technology to gather information and to adapt the environment so that it suits us. The other creatures of the world are one with nature. Instead of seeking to adapt the universe to suit them, they live in harmony with their surroundings. We, on the other hand, do not follow our natures but have dedicated our lives completely to rational thought. The problem with this is that rationality was never meant to be a guide through life. The function of the rational mind is to be a problem-solver. When a problem arises, the mind separates it into its various components and seeks to find the defective part. When the cause of the problem is discovered it can be dealt with. This process is fine for problem-solving but disastrous when used as a guide for life. The mind always separates. If we approach life rationally, we will not be able to see the Oneness of the universe, but only its separate parts.

Because we do approach life with the rational mind, we see ourselves as separate from nature. Hence, we think we can destroy nature without harming ourselves. We see ourselves separated from each other by nationality, age, race, religion, wealth, and so on. We have categorised everything and everybody. As a result, our lives are lived in isolation and loneliness. We have lost our feeling of Oneness with nature and with each other. The mind has created an identity for this separation that it has given rise to. This false separation is called the ego.

Even more tragic than our separation from the world is our separation from ourselves. We all know people who take care of their minds but ignore their bodies and vice versa. For such people the mind and the body cannot co-ordinate. How many times have you stood in the kitchen slicing tomatoes for supper? Where was your mind? What was your soul feeling? Were you aware of the feel of the knife against the palm of your hand? Did you feel the texture of the tomato as the knife sliced through it? Were you aware of how your hips, shoulder, abdomen, and wrist aided the hand in the slicing process? Did your soul feel the joy of preparing food that would nourish the life within yourself and others?

The answer to all these questions is, probably, no. Chances are that at the same time as you were cutting the tomato, you were thinking about the party next Friday night, watching a rerun of Dallas on television, and yearning for a more exciting life. Your body was in the kitchen slicing tomatoes, your mind was at a future party, your eyes and ears were in Dallas. Where were you? You were not 100 per cent 'here and now'. But here and now are the only place and time that exist. If you are not 100 per cent here and now, you are not 100 per cent alive.

Naturally, this separation from ourselves adds to our feeling of separation from others. Co-operation does not flourish in such an environment. Hence, the Western world has embraced competition rather than co-operation. From the very beginning, we are taught to compete. Our schools continue the competitive outlook on life that we instil in our children. Parents push their children to make the highest grades, win awards, etc. Everything is a contest. And there is no break from competition after school. Business companies are looking for aggressive young men and women who can compete with the aggressive young men and women of the other companies.

Even our religions are competitive: examine the divisions within the Christian faith. Even our love, even the sexual act, has become rooted in competition: 'Did I do O.K.?' 'Was she any good?' 'Did you enjoy it as much with me as you did with your previous boyfriend?'

Individual countries in the West compete on an economic basis. Our world might seem almost comical except that part of this competitive spirit is channelled into the arms race. Nations vie with one another to have the most destructive power. With the advent of nuclear weapons, war has become the ultimate competition. This is the point beyond which we cannot go. This is the point where our reliance on competition becomes a death-wish.

2
Tai Chi

As an answer to the condition of separation and conflict in which humanity finds itself, the Chinese developed a group of physical exercises combined with spiritual development which would aid the practitioner in obtaining an intuitive (as opposed to rational) understanding of, and Oneness with, the Tao. These physical disciplines are known collectively as 'Tai Chi'.

The Chinese saw that the continuous movement of the Tao follows certain principles. Through close observation of the world around them they discerned these principles and incorporated them into Tai Chi. The movements of Tai Chi are an imitation of the movements of the Tao. By imitating the Tao, the Tai Chi student becomes one with it, and harmonises himself with all things.

Tai Chi is an oriental discipline. That means that it must be done totally with all one's being in a process where the distinction between mind, soul, and body is lost as they flow into each other and merge in harmony. It must be a process where consciousness is dispersed from the mind throughout every cell of the body, so that the entire being becomes pure awareness. Hand, foot, breath, balance, and concentration blend into each other until the individual disappears into the void that is the Tao. In the Void, the ego is no more. There is only spontaneous, unceasing, harmonious movement.

Hence, Tai Chi is an unending journey toward oneself and toward Oneness with all things. It is a way of life that demands the most exquisite self-examination and a total awareness of what is happening around us. The Tai Chi student does not approach the world as it should be, or as he wishes it to be, but as it truly is. His or her task is to pierce the veil of prejudices and mind-sets of the society in which he or she was brought up in order to have a clear vision of the way things are.

The ancient Chinese classic *The Tao Te Ching* contains the ideas and principles from which the Tai Chi disciplines were derived. The following chapter will be an examination of selected verses of *The Tao Te Ching* in an attempt to present to the Tai Chi student these basic ideas and principles and to show how they are realised in Tai Chi practice.

All the passages quoted are taken from *The Tao Te Ching*, translated by Gia-Fu Feng, and published by Random House Inc., New York. There are a number of excellent translations of *The Tao Te Ching*, but I feel that Feng's work is the most rewarding for Tai Chi students. Feng is a Tai Chi teacher and directs the Stillpoint Foundation, a Taoist centre. His choice of words makes it easy to see how the ideas of *The Tao Te Ching* find their application in Tai Chi, and I strongly recommend that every serious Tai Chi student acquire a copy of Feng's translation.

3
Tai Chi and
The Tao Te Ching

Verse 1

In verse 1, the sage Lao Tzu (c.604–530 BC) describes the universe as an infinitely complex totality that the rational mind cannot grasp. To speak of the Tao is not to speak of the true Tao because the Tao is not something that can be put into words. You can only experience the Oneness of it. Tai Chi is an imitation of the Tao. It, too, is something that cannot be grasped by the mind. Tai Chi has to be experienced. You have to understand the Tao and Tai Chi with your total being; you have to grasp them with all your sense, your intuition, your inner awareness.

Ever desireless, one can see the mystery.

By 'desireless', Lao Tzu means that you must be without attachment. If you become attached to individual objects (money, motor cars, and so forth) or to individual people, you cannot see the Oneness that flows through all things, you only see the separate objects and people. But when you remain unattached, you can see the individual's Oneness with the rest of the universe. In other words, we see the world through the tinted glasses of our desires. If I see someone as a threat to the economic security that I desire, it will be very difficult for me to see the common humanity that binds us. By not seeing this brotherhood, I can treat him as separate from myself, which in turn means I can compete with him and have conflict with him. Thus, I see him through the shade of my desires and not as he is.

Ever desiring, one can see the manifestations:
These two spring from the same source but differ in name;
this appears as darkness.
Darkness within darkness.
The gate to all mystery.

In other words, the manifestations, the individual objects, all come from the same source, the Tao, and differ only in name. In reality, there is no difference. This individuality and oneness existing at the same time is the underlying mystery of all existence; a mystery for which the rational mind has no answer.

Tai Chi does not try to solve this mystery, we simply recognise it. Unlike other philosophies, Tai Chi thinking does not claim to have any ultimate answers to the mysteries of life. All that Tai Chi is concerned with is this moment, here and now. This is the only moment in which you exist. A second ago is no more and the second from now is not yet here. If you can move with the principles of the universe, which is the object of Tai Chi, you will become one with it and will have peace, tranquillity, and a harmonious life. All other questions, such as is there a god, is there life after death, etc., have no meaning for Tai Chi. Not only do we not know these things, but we cannot know them. The rational mind is limited, cannot grasp the infinite, and should make no claim to. Tai Chi does not know what the universe is, we only know how it works. In short, the Tao is a mystery.

The point of all this for the Tai Chi student is that you cannot practise Tai Chi with the rational mind. The most difficult thing for beginning students is that they try to make the movements with their minds and they cannot. The movements are too complicated. The flowing of the hands, the correct timing, the bending of the knees, the breathing, the balance; all this cannot be controlled by the mind. The pianist cannot think of each note as she plays it, it must simply be there. Just leave the body alone. When we do not interfere with it, the body moves with the Tao spontaneously.

The mystery of individuality and Oneness should be reflected in the Tai Chi class. The individuals should disappear into the Oneness of the class while at the same time maintaining and contributing their individual uniqueness to the shaping of the group movement. Thus, I should not open the door of the school and see Patricia, Thomas, etc. doing Tai Chi. I should open the door and see simply 'Tai Chi'. But I would experience the Tai Chi differently if Patricia was not there because her unique contribution to the harmony of the whole would be missing. In other words, I should not perceive individuals, but I should *feel* the absence of an individual.

Verse 2

Under heaven all can see beauty as beauty only because there is ugliness. All can know good as good only because there is evil.

Lao Tzu is saying that opposites cannot be separated. Within our traditional Western view, we see good and evil divided into two separate groups. Good is over here and bad is over there. But in Tai Chi thinking, good and bad cannot be separated. You cannot reject one and accept the other because the two are joined. The universe is not good. Nothing in and of itself is good or evil. Whether something is good or bad depends upon our relationship to that thing. We judge things according to our own desires, our own value systems. We say someone is beautiful according to our own personal or societal idea of what beauty is.

By calling things 'good' and 'bad', we divide the universe into two separate parts. Thus, the Oneness is lost. What Tai Chi advises is simply to accept things as they are without judging. As long as everything we perceive has to come through a filter of value judgements, we can never see things as they are. For example, if I think that all Kansans are ignorant, I will never meet an intelligent Kansan. No intelligent Kansan will be able to penetrate my prejudices.

Seeing things as they are is vital to a life of Tai Chi because we seek to become one with all things. Therefore, the Tai Chi student must be free of prejudice. What is Tai Chi? No one really knows. How would it be possible to judge between the good and the bad in Tai Chi? You cannot. The 98-year-old master who has been doing Tai Chi for eighty years is no 'better' than the student who began Tai Chi today. One of the most difficult problems connected with the learning of Tai Chi begins with the first few classes. The beginning classes work on flexibility, balance, breathing, and coordination. Some of the students do the exercises with no problems. Other students have a great deal of difficulty. Those who have difficulty see the students who have no problems and judge themselves as 'bad' students. They become discouraged and quit. The students who find the exercises easy and judge themselves as good often develop ego problems. But in Tai Chi, there is no such thing as good and bad. You are who you are. There is only one of you in the universe. I am John Lash. Am I a good John Lash or a bad John Lash? I don't know. There is no other John Lash to compare myself to. Is our sun a good sun or a bad sun? I don't know. It is the only sun we have. Thus, everything is individual and unique and cannot be compared to anything else. I cannot look at Mary to see if Sue is doing good Tai Chi. If I have a broken arm, it makes no difference to my arm if you are dying or if you simply have a headache. Whether I judge my situation good or bad does not matter, I still must get my arm taken care of. There is no sense in making comparisons.

Therefore the sage goes about doing nothing.

The idea of doing nothing is called 'Wu Wei' in Chinese. Wu Wei means to be without purpose, to act spontaneously. To act spontaneously is the only way the student can become one with the universe. The universe, the Tao, simply moves. It follows its nature according to its own principles. It flows effortlessly, without purpose, without a goal. Since Tai Chi is an imitation of the Tao, Tai Chi is also without a goal. Tai Chi is only Tai Chi when the student does it spontaneously and without purpose.

The Tai Chi person must move and act from his or her nature without purpose. For example, you come to my house and say, 'I am very hungry. Could you give me something to eat?' If my purpose is to be a good man (we are all brothers and sisters on this planet and it is my duty to share with this poor person), then I will give you something to eat. But this is not Wu Wei. I am trying to be a good man. I am trying to love my neighbour. And so I violate the Tao because I have a goal and an ambition which I am trying to impose on the universe.

On the other hand, if I act from my nature, I will give you the food not because I am trying to be a good man, but because I cannot deny a starving person. It would be contrary to my nature, to who I am, to say no. Thus, you would thank the good man because he is doing something good for you, but you would not thank me because I have no choice. It is my nature and I cannot say no. This is Wu Wei.

What Tai Chi is teaching you to do is to find your nature, who you are, so that you can live in that source. You must drop your pattern of ideas, judgements, goals, and ambitions and simply flow with your nature to where it takes you. The universe is a totality. Everything is essential to everything else. You are a unique person and the Tao would not be the Tao if you were not here. Thus, it is very important to the universe that you follow your nature to find your place and destiny in order to preserve the harmony of the whole.

How does Wu Wei apply to Tai Chi? To understand, you must ask yourself why you are studying Tai Chi, why you are practising it. Are you trying to lose weight? Or have you nothing to do on Tuesday nights and there is a Tai Chi class? Or what is it? If there is a reason, then what you are doing is not Tai Chi. You must train until the reason disappears and the Tai Chi flows from your nature. It is like riding the train to Houston not because you want to go to Houston, but because you enjoy the experience of riding a train and the train to Houston was the only one available. That is the way you have to do Tai Chi. That is Wu Wei. You are not interested in when or where you will eventually arrive. You are doing Tai Chi because it is your nature to do Tai Chi.

When your Tai Chi is without a goal, you become one with the movements and are no longer doing Tai Chi. You are Tai Chi. Thus, Tai Chi is not something you can do, it is something you must be.

Teaching no-talking.

Words cannot carry true knowledge. Only experience can give us knowledge. Hence, the Tai Chi person does not waste time talking unnecessarily. He knows he cannot help anyone by talking but only by example. Thus, Tai Chi is taught with movements rather than with books and lectures. The student must experience the Oneness of the universe through the uniting of the self with the movements. Words are useless. In Tai Chi, the student seeks to know with the complete being by using mind, body, and soul to experience Tai Chi.

The Tao is the Void from which all things come. The nature of a void is silence and emptiness. Tai Chi is an imitation of the Tao and for this reason must be done in silence. In silence, the mind naturally turns within to observe its own nature. This is one of the reasons that Westerners have so much fear of silence. Self-examination is sometimes alarming. We don't wish to uncover the pettiness and selfishness within ourselves. We might discover our true natures, who we really are, and realise that our destiny lies on an entirely different path from the way we have been travelling, and that to follow our true path might require great sacrifices.

The ten thousand things rise and fall without cease.

Ten thousand is a mystical number to the Chinese and is here used to mean everything that exists. What Lao Tzu is saying is that the universe is an infinite ocean of eternally flowing energy from which, through spontaneous mixing of the Yin and Yang Chis, objects appear. These manifestations of the Tao continue until the energies separate, and then they disappear back into the Void. Tai Chi imitates this flowing of the universe. Tai Chi is continuously flowing, rising into waves, sinking into troughs, eddying and swirling as the Yin and Yang combine and separate.

The last four lines of this verse describe how the Tao operates.

Creating, yet not possessing.

The Tao creates everything that exists, but it does not possess them. It makes no claim to ownership. The Tai Chi person follows this example. He creates, doing what must be done because it flows from his nature. But he remains unattached to that which he has created. As soon as the act of creation is finished, it is in the past and no longer here and now.

> *Working, yet not taking credit.*

The Tai Chi person only does that which comes from his nature, only that which he has to do. Why should he take credit for doing something he had no choice but to do? The Mississippi brings water to the people of New Orleans, but the people do not thank the river. The river brings water because that is the nature of a river. The Tai Chi person is the same as the river. He only does that which his nature demands that he do.

> *Work is done, then forgotten.*
> *Therefore it lasts forever.*

Because now it has become part of the Tao and nothing is ever lost from the Tao.

Verse 3

Not exalting the gifted prevents quarreling.

Competition is a separation, a loss of Oneness. Competition requires that there be two separate entities. If you compete with yourself, that simply demonstrates that you are separated from yourself. The Tai Chi life is built upon co-operation with all things. In Tai Chi self-defence, we co-operate with the other's strength rather than compete with it.

We co-operate with the world and thus we avoid conflict. There is no competition that is not harmful. If, for example, I won a competition and was named the world's best pianist, many other pianists would disagree with the verdict and resent me. To be exalted, to stand out, is a dangerous situation according to Tai Chi thinking. The Tai Chi person wants to blend into the universe and disappear so that he can fulfil his life without interference. To arouse envy endangers your harmony, tranquillity, and peace.

In traditional Chinese and Japanese paintings, there are always mountains, valleys, and rivers. Further, there is always a winding path through the mountains leading to a temple, and on this path is a little man. The mountains represent the Yang, or male principle of the universe. The valleys represent the female principle, Yin. The river represents the flow of the Chi energy through the world. The winding path is the Tao, the Way, Tai Chi. The path leads to a temple which represents oneness with the universe. The little man is the Tai Chi person on his journey. The little man is very difficult to see against the background of mountains and waterfalls, and you have to look very closely to pick him out, but he is always there. This is the Tai Chi person who has become so much one with the universe that he passes through life unnoticed. That is why there will never be a really famous Tai Chi person. If you should happen to meet a famous Tai Chi person, you know that something has gone badly wrong with his journey.

Tai Chi is not a competition. There are no awards, no trophies, no coloured belts of distinction. It has become a trend recently for some Tai Chi teachers to have their students take tests in order to judge the students' levels of advancement. Why tests? What kind of teacher is it that does not know how far his student has come? And, since Tai Chi is a never-ending process, what difference does it make anyway?

Some Tai Chi teachers encourage their students to enter martial arts competitions, like the international Tai Chi tournament in China. I remember a student telling me he was so proud because his teacher had won an international tournament. Yet, both teacher and student seem to have missed the point concerning what the essence of Tai Chi really is.

Not collecting treasures prevents stealing.

If you collect valuables (money, jewels, people, or whatever you consider valuable), you must eventually lose them. The universe is forever changing and everything must return to the Void from whence it came. There is nothing you can hang onto in the external world. Your partner could die; you could lose your money overnight. But there is one thing you can hold to, one thing that is never lost, the Chi centre. The universe, the Tao, is a circle which is always in motion. The only point that does not move is the infinitesimally small point at the centre. The universe moves around it, but the centre remains unmoving and unchanging.

It is the same situation with the Tai Chi person. As he moves through the storms and trials of life, as his body and mind change, as friends come and go, as grief and happiness alternate with each other, there remains within him an unmoving point, an island in a restless sea, that is ever peaceful, harmonious and tranquil. It is to this small point, the 'Tan Tien', the Chi centre approximately 2 inches below the navel, that the Tai Chi person clings, resting in its calmness safe from the turbulence flowing around him. So, hold to your centre. Avoid attachment to things outside yourself. If you collect objects of value, you will only cause envy. People will seek to take that which you value.

Not seeing desirable things prevents confusion of the heart.

When you have become one with your nature, when you are flowing with the currents of the universe, then the path that lies before you is clear. The path to the Tao is open. But if you have attachments, they will interfere with your ability to see clearly the direction that leads to Oneness. To travel to the Tao, something may have to be given up, such as the ego, a prejudice, or an ingrained world view. To reach your destiny, you must be willing to leap into the Void holding onto nothing but your own nature.

When you see anyone being mistreated, you know this is wrong. Everything is one and you cannot abuse another person without also abusing your own nature. But you may have some fear or desire that stands between you and this realisation (you might be worried in case this person takes your job) and therefore the desire to keep your economic and social status in society allows you to accept his mistreatment. Therefore, your attachment has come between you and your journey to the Tao.

The wise therefore rule by emptying hearts.

By 'emptying hearts', Lao Tzu means getting rid of attachments. You cannot help desiring things. It is human nature to have desires. But you must not become attached to the desire. You know you have become attached when you are willing to violate the Tao in order to obtain that which you desire.

...and stuffing bellies.

Simply take care of that which is necessary. All we really need is food, a place to sleep, and peace to develop in. All else is extra. Unfortunately, our economy is based upon creating desire for the extras. We have mass media and mass advertising to create desire after desire in order to keep the economy running. Our industry continuously invents new products for which we have no need, then spends millions of dollars on advertising to convince us that we *do* need these things. We are desire merchants and desire consumers. What we, as members of a society, should be doing is helping people to find happiness within themselves rather than seeking happiness in external objects.

By weakening ambitions.

The universe has no plan and no ambition. It is not going anywhere. It simply flows. It simply is. It simply flows where its nature takes it. When you bring your ambition into the ambitionless universe and try to force it upon the world, you are committing violence to the Tao and the harmony of the Oneness. You are attempting to force that which has no purpose to bend to your goal. You are trying to force me, to force everything, to accept your ambition. This leads to manipulation of people, society, and nature. The Tai Chi life is a life of co-operation.

And strengthening bones.

Again, Lao Tzu is saying to take care of that which is necessary and allow your nature to take you where you are supposed to be.

If people lack knowledge and desire,
then intellectuals will not try to interfere.

Lao Tzu uses the word 'knowledge' to mean that type of knowledge we call cunning (that is, the ability to connive and to manipulate people). In referring to intellectuals, he means people who, knowing what your attachments are, can use ideas and facts to manipulate you. If I know what it is you want and what it is that you are afraid of, then I know how to control you.

If nothing is done, then all will be well.

In other words, if nothing is done with purpose and ambition, if everything flows in a natural, spontaneous process, then everything works. Nature is the example. You do not have to interfere with nature. Nature works by itself simply following the principles of Tao. A tree has no ambition. Simply by following the nature of a tree, it lives in harmony with the rest of nature without doing anything. Thus, living in harmony with the universe does not require that you do something, but merely that you be.

Verse 4

The Tao is an empty vessel; it is used but never filled.

The Tao is emptiness, nothingness, the Void. From the Void comes all that is. Thus, our nature is emptiness. When we can unite our mind, body, and soul in the Tan Tien, our Chi centre, we are in the Void and one with all things. We can reach the Void by emptying ourselves of ego, ambition, attachment, and fixed ideas about the way the world is. When that is accomplished, we can face life with tranquillity, seeing the world as it truly is and not through the distorted glass of the ego.

The Japanese have probably developed this idea of emptiness to its highest form. The traditional Japanese house has little furniture and their Zen gardens are bare. On entering such a house or garden, one has the feeling of space, of freedom, of infinity, of serenity.

Western life is just the opposite. We clutter our lives up with possessions. We stuff our homes with furniture. It is very difficult for us to experience the feeling of emptiness. And we like it that way because we are afraid of the Void where there is no ego, no desires, but only ourselves and the vastness of the Tao. We identify ourselves with the ego and think that it is our ego that makes us special. We fear anything that threatens our vision of ourselves as pictured through the ego. But what really makes us unique is our inner nature. The ego is a fiction created by the rational mind to justify its usurpation of our lives. The ego is but a collection of desires, often artificially imposed from outside ourselves, and memories of past achievements and failures. We use the ego to separate ourselves from others in order to make ourselves feel important. Thus the Tai Chi student's task is to rid him- or herself of the ego in order to reach the Void.

The next lines are guides for a Tai Chi life. Where is the Tai Chi person going? He is moving towards Oneness with the universe and a life of harmony and tranquillity where there is no separation from or conflict with others. His life is a reflection of the Tao.

Untangle the knot.

Simplify whatever there is within you that is complicated. If you have enough to eat and a place to sleep, that is enough for you to live a life of Tao. But the mind is a problem-solver. If there are no problems, the mind will create them. And the more complicated the problem, the more interesting it is. The ego wants life to be a drama and it wants to be the star. For some people, when a stranger sits beside them on the bus and says, 'Good morning,' the mind already begins a problem-solving process. Why did he or she say that? What does he or she want? That is why in Western society most people ride on public transport in total silence.

This complicating process is readily seen in the Tai Chi class. Tai Chi movements are really very simple but beginning students insist upon making Tai Chi difficult by adding extra moves. I am often amazed at the mistakes people make because the mistake is much more difficult to make than the correct move. Tai Chi is not complicated; people are complicated.

Soften the glare.

Get rid of that about you which shines forth so brightly that it causes discomfort to others. We have all met people who dominate conversation, or who always try to push themselves forward by proclaiming their accomplishments, talents, etc. Such behaviour only causes resentment and leads to conflict. The Tai Chi person must merge with the Tao and be as humble as the dust. The talents and accomplishments of such a person will cause no resentment.

Oh, hidden deep but ever present.

The Tao, and its harmony, are hidden within us by the falseness of the ego, but they are always there to be drawn upon. In moments of emptiness and silence, we can feel it. That is why the student feels so peaceful after doing the Tai Chi moves. When the movements are completed, the whole class stands silent and unmoving for minutes at a time. This is not something the teacher teaches the students, but a natural desire of the students to remain in the soothing embrace of the deeply felt peace evoked by the movements.

I do not know from whence it comes.

No one knows how the feeling of peace and tranquillity is brought forth by the Tai Chi movements. There are no rational or scientific answers. And we do not seek to know. The reasons are unimportant. All that matters is that this peaceful centre is there and can be reached through Tai Chi.

Verse 5

Heaven and earth are ruthless;
they see the ten thousand things as dummies.
The wise are ruthless;
they see the people as dummies.

By stating, 'Heaven and earth are ruthless', Lao Tzu means that the universe is impartial. The universe follows certain principles in its movement. As long as you are in accord with these principles, the universe provides all you need. But if you violate the principles of the universe, you will be crushed. The universe is like a river. The river cannot leave its nature. It must follow the principles of water. As long as you understand the principles of water and adjust your behaviour to them, everything works very well. You can quench your thirst, you can grow your crops, you can wash your clothes, you can fish for food, and you can swim. These actions are possible because this is the nature of a river. However, if you violate the principles of water, if you pollute it, or if you jump into the river with lead boots on, the river will kill you, because it has no choice.

The Tai Chi person is like the river. This person, too, must be impartial, and treat all people the same. As I said before, if you are hungry, I will give you something to eat, not because I like you, or because I am a good man, but because I have no choice. It is not in my nature to deny a starving person. On the other hand, if you were hurting my children, then I would hurt you, not because I do not like you, but because I have no choice. It would be impossible for me to stand by while you harmed my children, whether you were my best friend or a total stranger. My action would be impartial.

The space between heaven and earth is like a bellows.

The flowing of Yin and Yang through the Tao is the breath of the universe. As in the macrocosm, so in the microcosm. Tai Chi breathing is an imitation of the Great Breath of the Tao. Thus, correct breathing is one of the basic aspects of Tai Chi. It is part of tuning ourselves to the rhythm of the Tao. The Tai Chi breath must be deep and full, spontaneous and natural, and in accordance with the Yin and Yang movements of the body. The ability to increase breath capacity is one of the many health benefits that come with the practice of Tai Chi. It is a benefit that becomes progressively more important as the body ages. Breath is life. More breath is more life.

The shape changes but not the form.

The shape of the universe is always changing as the universe moves, but the principles these movements follow never change. The movements in Tai Chi continuously change but the principles that dictate each move are unchanging. When these principles are finally learned and become ingrained in the student's life, he or she will need no teacher. The student will be able to correct his/her own movements.

The more it moves, the more it yields.

Yielding is the way of Tao. By yielding, we avoid the petty conflicts that sometimes seem to take up most of our lives. If someone comes to work in an angry mood and says something bad to you, yield. Do not respond angrily. That would only increase his anger. If such an exchange continues, open conflict results. It is better to yield. Anger must have something strong to hit against. If there is no response, no feed-back, anger dissipates. Yielding may hurt the ego, but the ego has no place in Tai Chi.

More words count less.

Words and ideas cannot grasp truth. Truth can only be experienced. It is in silence that we most easily experience the harmony and peace of the Tao. Our Western societies draw ever further away from this ideal of silence. We are overwhelmed by noise pollution which keeps us from being able to relax and which wreaks havoc on our nervous systems. Like emptiness, silence is something we fear because in silence the soul automatically looks inward. We fear what we shall see there and the revelations about the kind of person we are. Noise is our way of avoiding such introspection. Many people are so uncomfortable in the absence of noise that they will leave the television on even when no one is watching it. I have passed people on lonely mountain paths carrying radios that were blasting out rock music. They like the mountain scenery but fear the silence.

Tai Chi is a silent discipline and should be practised in a quiet place. This quietness will aid the student's concentration and allow him to sink more easily into his centre. Ultimately, the student must learn to carry his own silence with him wherever he goes. When he can establish the silence within himself, he will not be distracted by the meaningless noise around him. But such an ability requires a great deal of practice. Thus, the beginning student should have as quiet a place as possible in which to learn.

Verse 6

*The valley spirit never dies;
It is the woman, primal mother.*

The valley is a symbol of Yin Chi, the female principle of the universe. The Tao is female, the Mother of all that exists. Thus, Tai Chi is the way of the female. The Tai Chi student follows this female path, and becomes like the valley where all things are nourished. By becoming non-aggressive, non-violent, yielding, and weak he achieves union with the mother.

Her gateway is the root of heaven and earth.

This is another example of the female as a symbol of the Tao and of Tai Chi. 'Her gateway', the vagina, is empty and circular like the Tao. Everything that exists comes from the gateway of the Tao. Every person that exists comes from the gateway of the female. Men have a natural advantage in such disciplines as karate and kung-fu. In Tai Chi, the natural advantage can be seen to lie with the female. Women are naturally more flexible and yielding than men because women have less muscular strength. Flexibility must always be traded for a gain in muscle size. Tai Chi works with the joints in order to increase flexibility and uses Chi energy rather than muscles for power. Thus, the more muscular the student is, the more difficulty he will have with the movements. Tai Chi is definitely no place for a man with a 'macho' outlook on life.

It is like a veil barely seen.

It is very difficult to see the Oneness in our world of separation and competition, just as it is difficult for the beginner to feel the Oneness of the Tai Chi movements when he is just beginning. But in both cases the Oneness is there. You only need to become sensitive to it. The practice of Tai Chi aids the student to pierce the veil.

Use it; it will never fail.

When the student realises his Oneness with the universe and tunes himself to it, the Oneness will never fail him. It will become the centre of his life and his refuge in times of trouble.

Verse 8

The highest good is like water.
Water gives life to the ten thousand things and does not strive.
It flows in places men reject and so is like the Tao.

Water, along with the female and the infant, is a symbol of Tai Chi. As such, the Tai Chi person patterns his life upon its characteristics. Water is absolutely essential for our existence. It nourishes our bodies and our world, and yet asks for nothing in exchange. Though it has such an important role in the life of the world, it seeks the lowest places and flows there in humility. Water is soft and yielding, and yet overcomes the rock in its path. With its weakness, it cuts mighty canyons through the mountains. It does not compete or strive, it makes no effort, it has no goal, but simply flows to where its nature takes it: the ocean.

Like water, the Tai Chi person gives of himself to everyone whom he meets without judging between the good and the bad, or the deserving and the undeserving. He seeks the lowest places in life and in his humbleness, he neither strives with the world, nor attacks it with his ambitions. He overcomes strength with the weakness of his compassion and mercy.

In dwelling, be close to the land.

This is very difficult advice to follow in the modern, industrialised nations that make up the Western world. Most of us have to dwell in the city to make a living. Thus, we do not get up with the sun, nor do we go to sleep with the darkness as the rest of the creatures of the world do. We have developed artificial light so that we can stay up late seeking entertainment. All day we walk on concrete and asphalt, and we forget the feel of the earth. We have lost our knowledge of how to adapt ourselves to nature, how to be one with it. When we visit the countryside on our vacations, we bring the city along with our noise and our exhaust fumes. We leave our rubbish as a parting gift to the beauty that beckoned us. Rather than adapting to nature, we make nature adapt to us and, by so doing, we destroy it.

The perfect example of our separateness from nature can be found in the desert communities of the United States, such as Phoenix, Arizona and Albuquerque, New Mexico. People move to these places from the northern parts of the US in order to enjoy the warm, sunny climates. Unfortunately, they ignore the fact that they are moving to a totally different environment from the forests and well-watered lands that they are used to. They feel no need to adapt themselves to their new surroundings.

The Indians and Mexican-Americans of the southwest have lived for centuries in houses made of adobe. These thick-walled houses composed of mud and straw are warm in the winter and cool in the heat of the desert summer. The newly arrived northerner, however, wants to live in a brick and board house like the one he lived in when he resided in New York or Michigan. Such houses are unbearably cold in the winter and too hot in the summer. Thus, the newcomer must use large quantities of heating fuel and he must install an air-conditioner. Air-conditioners require a lot of water.

The newcomer is also used to green lawns with trees. The fact that he lives in a brown and treeless desert means nothing to him. As a result, precious water is used to create a New York lawn. The real estate developers build him an artificial lake so that he can go fishing on the weekend like he used to do in the north, and ignore the fact that as much as 40 per cent of the lake's water is evaporated every day by the desert sun, therefore requiring the continuous pumping in of water. These developers know that the northerner does not want to play golf on a brown course and so the sprinklers are kept working all day. Such development in a desert must lead to disaster. Already, the states of Arizona and New Mexico are running out of water. Such an attitude towards satisfying desires at any cost spells disaster for us all.

The Tai Chi person should spend as much time with nature as possible so that he can learn its ways and adapt to its rhythms. I often tell my students that if they want to improve their Tai Chi they should go to the zoo and spend a few hours watching the cranes, or sit by the river observing the flow of the current.

In meditation, go deep in the heart.

Tai Chi is a moving meditation in which we go deep into the heart rather than deep into the mind. The universe is too vast for the mind to grasp. But in the heart lie compassion, love, and mercy. The heart has a limitless capacity for love and thus can encompass the limitless Tao. Love, compassion, and mercy are the only qualities that can make us one with others, and are the very essence of Tai Chi.

In dealing with others, be gentle and kind.

To harm you, is to harm myself; to be kind to you is to be kind to myself.

In speech, be true.

Be as truthful as you can, but understand the nature of truth. Truth is something that changes with viewpoints. Am I tall? It depends upon whether you are an ant, or a tree. Hold to the truth as you see it while always remembering that there are many other views.

In ruling, be just.

Develop the ability to see clearly and do not allow attachment to an idea or a person or a possession to sway your judgement.

In business, be competent.

Whatever it is that you are doing, do it 100 per cent. You are only 100 per cent alive when you are 100 per cent here and now. Usually we judge how important an activity is by what the result of that activity will be. And, on that basis, we judge how important a person is by the activity he performs. But the Tai Chi person is not interested in results. Results are in the future and the Tai Chi person lives in the here and now. Cutting a tomato for supper can be seen as being just as important as performing brain surgery, or playing a piano in a concert. Why should our lives only feel full when we are doing something our society judges important? When everything you do becomes important, your life will be full of meaning. When we approach life this way, then everyone is equal. The dustman is just as valuable as the scientist. The Tao does not judge among people or activities, and neither does the Tai Chi person.

In action, watch the timing.

In the Western world, we go through life trying to force things to be the way we want them to be, rather than waiting for the correct moment to act. Tai Chi, on the other hand, teaches the student that he cannot force his way through life. Patience is an essential requirement of Tai Chi. Tai Chi is an unending journey through an infinite universe, so what is the hurry? A student once came to his Tai Chi master and asked, 'How long will it take me to learn Tai Chi well?' The master said, 'Ten years.' Then the student inquired, 'What if I try twice as hard as everyone else?' The master answered, 'Then, it will take you twenty years.'

In Tai Chi self-defence, we do not use our strength and speed to try and force our way through the attacker's defence in order to strike. We avoid and yield until the correct second to strike. We wait until the attacker has become over-extended and off-balance. When these conditions are present, we move instantly with all of our power and concentration. This is called, 'waiting for the Tao'. This philosophy applies to everything we do in life, not just self-defence. If you are relaxed, tranquil, flexible, and centred within yourself, you can move at any time in any direction with all of your power.

Because of the importance of 'timing', Tai Chi is designed to perfect this ability. All the movements require that the hand, foot, knee, etc., begin at the same second and reach the point of completion at the same second. Sometimes, the hand has a much longer way to travel than the knee, but they must still begin and finish at the same second. This means that the hand and knee must move at different speeds. This is not something that the mind can control. You cannot think the correct speed for the different parts of the body. It is the body itself that must know the correct speed. Because of our training our body is in close touch and harmony with our will. Thus, the body 'knows' of itself where it is going and, because of this, the hand knows at what speed it is required to move in order to arrive with the knee. When your body, mind, and soul have become one in this manner, you will go through life knowing when to act and when to 'wait for the Tao'.

No fight: No blame.

If you do not compete, if you do not quarrel, then no blame can be attached to you and you will never be resented. This allows you to move toward your destiny and the fulfilment of your nature peaceably.

Verse 9

Better stop short than fill to the brim.
Oversharpen the blade, and the edge will soon blunt.
Amass a store of gold and jade, and no one can protect it.
Claim wealth and titles, and disaster will follow.

The message of the above lines is not to go too far. Opposites cannot be separated. If you go far enough in one direction, you cross over into the opposite of where you want to go. If you are doing a Yang move in Tai Chi, you want the knee to stop its forward movement when it arrives in line with the toe. Yang moves are for the sending forth of power. The maximum amount of power is delivered when the knee lines up with the toe. Going further than the toe changes a Yang move into a Yin move, which lessens the amount of power delivered because Yin moves are for conserving power. Hence, you get the opposite of what you seek by going too far.

This same principle guides all aspects of life. Eating ice cream is a pleasure until I go too far. People desire great sums of money for the freedom and pleasure it will bring into their lives, but there is a certain point where money limits pleasure and freedom. When they reach a point where wealth makes them famous, their privacy is lost and consequently their freedom is curtailed. And we have all seen boxers or other athletes who compete for too long and receive the opposite of the success and victory they are striving for. One must know when to stop.

Retire when the work is done.

Again, know when to stop. But only retire after the work is done, only after you have done what your nature moved you to do.

This is the way of heaven.

To act and then withdraw is the way of the Tao, and the way of Tai Chi. Do what your nature requires you to do without regard to whether your action receives praise or condemnation from society. What is done is done and the Tai Chi person lives only in the here and now.

Verse 10

*Carrying body and soul and embracing the one,
Can you avoid separation?*

The Tai Chi person must unify his body, mind, soul, and nature so that he can pass through life with 100 per cent awareness, ready to adapt to and respond to any situation with all of his power and ability. We are born with this unification and lose it as we grow older and become separated from ourselves. A baby is weak, and yet has an incredible amount of strength. Try taking a toy away from an infant. He holds it so tightly that you can pick the child up off the floor by lifting the toy. Where does this strength come from? The child has no muscles. It comes from the child focusing his will and uniting it with all the energy of his soul and body. This ability comes naturally to children and animals. Try holding a small frog in your hands. The frog wriggles and pushes until he squeezes out through the fingers. Babies and frogs do not give up. They cannot because they have no rational minds to intervene between the will and the rest of themselves. The rational mind cannot tell them that the situation is hopeless or that the body is too weak. They will an action and then proceed to fulfil that action with all their being.

Only when the rational mind does not interfere with the natural functioning of our Oneness can we realise our full potential in life. Thus, we can see what the human body is capable of when the mind does not interfere. It is possible for a mother to lift a car off her injured child. The emotional distress short-circuits the rational process that would inform her that she is not capable of lifting a car. We see it with people who are hypnotised and with the insane. Hypnotised people can perform amazing feats of physical strength; the police dislike dealing with an insane person because his strength seems to have increased tenfold. In both these cases the rational mind has lost its ruling influence.

Hence, the infant, the animal, the person under great stress, the hypnotised, and the insane have this ability to 'embrace the one' because the rational mind does not separate their total beings into mind–body–soul–will. Tai Chi seeks to recover this natural ability. In Tai Chi, we sink the rational mind into the Chi centre, the Tan Tien, relegating it to its one and only function as a problem-solver. The teacher can see when the student has developed the capacity to do this. The student will struggle along with the moves, perhaps for years, trying to use the mind to control the body. But then will come the point where the student is overcome by the futility of his efforts and allows the body to flow from within itself. It is then that real Tai Chi begins.

Attending fully and becoming supple,
Can you be as a newborn babe?

A baby is flexible in mind and body. It has little muscular strength to restrict the fluidity of its movements, and it has no set ideas about the way the world is. Thus, it can adapt and adjust to any situation. To do Tai Chi, the student must have this flexibility of mind and body. In my school, we spend the first two months in beginners classes working on flexibility, and the first part of every class after that as long as the student remains in the school. Though physical flexibility requires a great deal of patience to develop, more students leave Tai Chi because of mental inflexibility. They cannot give up life-long prejudices and ways of looking at the world.

Washing and cleansing the primal vision,
Can you be without stain?

We see the world with distorted vision. Our vision has been distorted by prejudices and ideas of right and wrong. We see only what we already have in our minds and not what is truly there. When you empty yourself of fixed opinions, attachments, and ego, the mesh of ideas and prejudices through which we view life is destroyed. The Tai Chi student must drop everything and be as a mirror that reflects things as they are.

Loving all men and ruling the country,
Can you be without cleverness?

Love is the only thing that can make us one with others. Love is the only force that unites individuals. And it is only through Oneness that our natures can develop to the fullest. Love is the one essential requirement for the student of Tai Chi. Being rooted in love allows the student to pass through life without manipulating others.

Opening and closing the gates of heaven,
Can you play the role of woman?

At the beginning of the sexual act, the woman is weak and pliant. The man is hard and strong. After the sexual act, the man is weak and soft. Through her weakness, softness, and yieldingness, the woman takes away the strength and aggression of the man while remaining unchanged. The Tai Chi person follows the role of the female by using weakness and softness to overcome strength and aggression. In Tai Chi self-defence, this is done by allowing the aggressor to commit his strength in a certain direction, then yielding and bringing him into a position of weakness. Thus, we rob him of his strength and nullify his aggression.

Understanding and being open to all things,
Are you able to do nothing?

Understanding the principles upon which the universe operates, ridding ourselves of the fiction of the ego, and dropping our prejudices, we can open ourselves to all things. We can be open because we will fear nothing. It is only when we are without fear that we can *do* nothing. Without fear, we can react to everything spontaneously and openly.

Giving birth and nourishing...

The Tai Chi student gives birth to a new way of life for himself and, by being an example, opens this new way of life to others. In the process, he becomes all things to all people. He helps everyone and everything to find its nature and thus nourishes all whom he meets. Because of his sensitivity, he can feel the needs of others. He can be a father to the fatherless, a brother to the brotherless, a teacher to those who need a teacher, etc. He becomes an Earth Father, loving all existence as a father loves his son. The student can be an Earth Father or an Earth Mother through the absence of fear, which allows the student to be open to all without judging them.

Bearing yet not possessing...

The Tai Chi person has possessions but makes sure they do not possess him by remaining unattached to them.

Leading yet not dominating...

The leadership of the Tai Chi person leads to a world of peace and harmony, and relies solely upon example.

Verse 11

Thirty spokes share the wheel's hub;
It is the centre hole that makes it useful.
Shape clay into a vessel;
It is the space within that makes it useful.

Everything arises from the Tao. The Tao is a Void, emptiness, non-being. This nothingness, this emptiness, is the very essence, the centre of everything that exists. It is this link of emptiness that makes all things one. Thus, when we root ourselves in the Void, we enter a place where all things meet. In the Void lie harmony, tranquillity and peace. There can be no conflict where all things are united in Oneness.

In the highest levels of the martial arts, the practitioner seeks to enter the Void and remain there because as long as he is in the Void, he is one with the attacker and cannot be harmed. If you go to see a Japanese sword-fighting competition, you will see the young students standing opposite each other with their sword-points touching. When the judge signals, the two contestants begin to swing their swords, fighting, jumping, twisting, seeking to force an opportunity to strike the opponent. The contest ends when one of the two has gathered three points.

However, at such a contest, you may have the opportunity to see two old masters. They touch the points of their swords together and wait for the judge to signal. When the signal comes, they will remain motionless, waiting. After a certain period of time, the judge will declare the contest a draw. What has happened is that the two masters realise that their opponent is in the Void, and thus it is useless to strike at him. When someone is in the Void, all that can be done is to try to bring him out. This can be done by making him angry, appealing to his ego, or in some other way causing him to lose his harmony. Only then can you strike. Otherwise, it is useless to jump around swinging your sword.

Usually when doing the Tai Chi form, the student concentrates fully upon every detail of each move. But, with practice, the time will come when the student passes over into the Void. He will find himself at the end of the sequence of moves and realise that he was not consciously moving, that he does not remember doing the moves. The moves were coming from within himself spontaneously without the interference of the mind. In other words, he was in the Void and one with the Tai Chi.

> *Therefore profit comes from what is there;*
> *Usefulness from what is not there.*

Everything extra in life, everything which is more than we actually need, comes from being individual, separated objects. If something is separate from us, we can use it for profit, including people. These unnecessary things, such as expensive clothes, fancy cars, jewellery, servants, etc. are only to enhance the ego. But life, true existence, is in the Void. When we become one with things and people, we no longer use them, we are them and move with them spontaneously. That is why Tai Chi must not be a discipline separate from ourselves, but internal movements that we are.

Verse 12

The five colours blind the eye.
The five tones deafen the ear.
The five flavours dull the taste.
Racing and hunting madden the mind.

When not involved in problem-solving, the mind should be still and at rest. The result of our not knowing who we really are, of being separated from our own nature, is that we make the mistake of identifying ourselves with the mind. The ego is this false identification. The rational mind is an insatiable information-gatherer. Thus, it always wants to be fed, and constantly seeks new data. Since the rational mind is in control, it does not cease its problem-solving functions even when the body needs rest. Hence, insomnia is one of the largest problems in our society. And, when it has no problem to dwell on, it will create problems in order to keep busy. Go sit in the mountains sometime and look at the majesty all around, and you will soon see that most of your problems are not real.

The mind is a tyrant that must be constantly entertained. Through the senses, it draws us ever further away from ourselves by its attraction to the outer world. It does not like silence and self-examination. Our modern, urban societies are designed to provide us with constant entertainment. When a visitor comes to see us, we go to a movie, or to a restaurant, etc. We never just do nothing. And, when we are alone, bored, and restless, we turn on the television, sit there and watch it for hours.

We fear to be with one another in silence. I have a friend who comes to my farm to visit me occasionally. We live quite a distance apart from each other, so the visits are pretty rare. When he arrives, he begins to talk and he talks for the entire visit. But there is so much work to do on a farm, chopping wood, making hay, cleaning stalls, etc., and I do not have time to sit for hours talking.

And, being a Tai Chi person, I do not have a lot to say. He always leaves disappointed and says that he will come some other time when I do not have so much work to do. How much better it would be if he came in silence. We would chop wood together with not a word spoken, simply feeling the warmth of the companionship that develops with shared work. In the silence, we could see how it is with each other, feel the pain, sadness, or joy without the mediation of the ego's words, allow our minds to rest and find tranquillity. On parting, a simple, sincere embrace to communicate the love we feel for each other and the joy of our friendship would be the best farewell.

Therefore the sage is guided
by what he feels
and not by what he sees.

The Tai Chi person is guided by his intuitive knowledge, by what he grasps from life as a whole, rather than by his mind. If your car will not start, the mind automatically divides the problem into its separate components. Intuitive knowledge, on the other hand, is not a separating kind of knowledge. It unites separate things into a totality. For example, say that I have a waste-disposal problem at my chemical factory. The mind goes to work looking at the separate facts:

1. There are no landfills nearby.
2. Transportation is expensive.
3. There is a river within a short distance.

The answer: dump the waste in the river. True, this is the answer to an individual, isolated problem. However, I intuitively know the answer is wrong because of my abiding love for nature as a whole and my compassion for humanity. I know with my whole being that this dumping of waste into the river is wrong. I do not need to understand the health problems rationally, nor do I need a scientific description of how the environment will be harmed. I *know* from within myself. When rational knowledge is separated from love and compassion, disaster must follow. Intuitive knowledge must be our guide through life.

He lets go of that and chooses this.

The Tai Chi person must let go of the things outside himself. That does not mean that you do not see and enjoy external things, it means that you do not become attached to them. You choose this, your own centre, which is within you. The Tai Chi person can only remain attached to his own centre.

The universe is like a great ocean. Sometimes the waters whip around you in hurricane storms. In this violent sea, there is nothing to cling to but your own centre. When this ability to be fixed to your centre is developed, you can remain unmoved in the midst of catastrophes. When the world around you collapses, you alone will stand. People in trouble will be drawn to you. They will be able to hold to you because you will have become the rock in the storm, the centre of the Tao.

One of the most common problems in self-defence is that people tend to panic when an attack is directed toward them. Or they tense up so much that they can no longer function with the Chi. In Tai Chi, the idea is to relax in the face of danger. When the body is relaxed and the mind is at peace, flexibility is heightened and the Chi can flow freely. This ability requires a great deal of peace and harmony within the individual, and comes only when the student rests in his centre.

Verse 13

What do you mean by 'Accept disgrace willingly'?
Accept being unimportant.

Since the ego considers itself the centre of everything, the idea that we are unimportant is probably the hardest thing in our lives to accept. What Lao Tzu is saying is that we should accept being unimportant to other egos. The Tai Chi person may go through life completely unknown and unnoticed. Indeed, this is the best situation for him as he seeks to move through life following his nature unhindered.

However, you are vitally important to other natures. The universe is a totality and its harmony depends upon each individual part finding its nature and following that nature to its destiny. When one piece of existence does not do this, the harmony of the Oneness is lost. In other words, if you were absent the Tao would cease to exist. That being the case, why should great honour or great disgrace have any meaning for you? Neither the blame nor the applause of the world of egos should be allowed to distract you from doing that which you have to do in order to follow your nature to where it leads you.

What do you mean by 'Accept misfortune as
the human condition'?
Misfortune comes from having a body.
Without a body, how could there be misfortune?

Misfortune is part of the human condition. Because of the nature of the human body, we have desires, many of which can never be fulfilled. This fact, however, can only cause us misfortune if we are attached to the objects of our desires. Attachment is the willingness to abandon the path down which our nature is leading us in order to obtain the object of our desire. This loss of our oneness with our true selves is the greatest of misfortunes. Without attachment, there can be no misfortune because, whether we obtain the object of our desire or not is irrelevant. If the Tai Chi person cannot have what he desires, he simply releases it and moves on with the never-ending flow of his nature.

Most people have a very strong attachment to the well-being of the body. This attachment gives us a great fear of death. Fear of death can cause us to abandon our path when to follow it would lead us into danger. However, if you are not attached to your body, it cannot be a misfortune to lose it. To be a true Tai Chi person, the student must give up his attachment to the body because the Tai Chi journey requires fearlessness.

If the Tai Chi student has no compassion and is unwilling to defend the helpless, he will never be a true Tai Chi person. If the student does have compassion and willingness, they can be cancelled by the fear of death. Thus, to be completely free to act as his nature requires, he must be without fear. Even death is preferable to violating your own humanity. Fear, whether for the loss of your family, your money, or your life, comes from attachment. Without attachment, there cannot be fear.

Surrender yourself humbly;
then you can be trusted to care for all things.

Help to others must only be given because it comes from your nature. There cannot be any motive. You help someone because you have no other choice; your nature demands it. If you are helping me because you seek wealth or fame or to be good, you will abandon me as soon as you see that these things come from a different direction. This is the way of most politicians.

Live a life of humility, seeing yourself as the servant of all things and all people. Be the unnoticed caretaker of the universe. When the world sees your humility and realises that you seek no personal gain, but are simply being who you are, it will trust you. All things and people will accept your aid with gladness.

Love the world as your own self;
then you can truly care for all things.

Love is the only thing that can make you one with another person or thing. Love is the essence of Tai Chi. Once you have reached the stage of being able to love all that is, then not only will you be trusted to care for the world, but you really can care for the world.

I know many people who preach love and non-violence, but when the USSR shot down a Korean airliner, these same people marched to the Russian embassy, threw stones and yelled curses. Anyone who would shoot down a civilian airliner has a sickness inside their soul and deserves compassion, not hatred.

If I believe that you hate me, why should I care if you disagree with my behaviour? But, if I know that you care about me, that you comprehend my fears and the difficulties I face in life, then I will be able to listen. At least with love, there is the chance that I will listen, but with hatred, there is no chance at all. Love comes from the heart whereas hatred comes from the ego. Hatred requires no sacrifice, no humility, and no self-awareness.

Verse 14

This verse is a description not only of the Tao, but also of the Tai Chi person.

> *Look, it cannot be seen...*
> *Listen, it cannot be heard...*
> *Grasp, it cannot be held...*

The Oneness that is the Tao is not something that can be seen. It is hidden in the myriad, individual manifestations of its parts. Likewise, the Tai Chi person cannot be seen because he has become one with all that is. He disappears into the Tao. Thus, in my school, it is required to wear black. Black is the colour of Yin, humility, invisibility, and mystery, all characteristics of the Tao. This helps the student disappear into the Oneness of the group as the movements flow. Watching the Tai Chi, I do not see Jim sticking out in a patterned T-shirt, or Mary in a brightly-coloured jogging suit. When the student is doing Tai Chi alone, it does not matter what he wears or how fast he moves, but in the class the individual must disappear into the whole.

The Tao is silent; it cannot be heard. It does not claim attention or fame even though it fulfils all our needs. Likewise, the Tai Chi student is silent, flowing in the Void, not making claims to fame. Hence, the Tai Chi school must be a place of emptiness and silence. Like the Tao, Tai Chi flows silently.

The Tao cannot be grasped with the mind. It is beyond rational understanding and can only be experienced. It is the same with Tai Chi. Tai Chi cannot be grasped with the mind, and thus is not something that can be studied. It is something you must feel. Beginning students always seek to grasp the movements with their mind. This causes no end of problems, but seems to be an unavoidable stage. Sooner or later the student reaches a level where the mind can no longer cope with the complexities of the movements; the student simply relaxes, and the body flows through the moves of its own accord. Only then is the student doing Tai Chi.

In Tai Chi self-defence, the Tai Chi person cannot be grasped. Weak and flexible as bamboo, flowing and yielding as water, the Tai Chi person offers no place to hold.

Stand before it and there is no beginning.

When does Tai Chi begin? Did you begin Tai Chi the second you were born, or even before that? Or did you begin when you took your first lesson? No one knows how far you have come on the path to the Tao. There is no way to judge because we each have our own unique path. In many of the martial arts, at the end of the lesson, the students bow to the teacher and then the teacher bows to the students. The students bow first because the teacher deserves respect for how far he has travelled on the journey. But in Tai Chi, at the end of the lesson, students and teacher bow at the same time because there is no one who can with certainty be judged to have gone further. Hence, the Tai Chi class is a group of equals. Like the student, the teacher must also disappear. The visitor to a Tai Chi class should not be able just to look in the door and recognise which person is the teacher.

Follow it and there is no end.

Tai Chi, like the universe, has no beginning and no end because it has no goal. The Tai Chi person is not going anywhere; he is simply being. The universe moves but it always remains here and now. When the last of the 108 moves of the Tai Chi Chuan have been completed, where has the student moved to? Nowhere. The student is exactly where he started. It is not a goal, but simply the process of moving that is important in Tai Chi. Because it has no goal, because there is nothing to achieve, Tai Chi is an endless journey.

Stay with the ancient Tao,
Move with the present.

Hold to your centre, to the Oneness, to the principles that have governed the universe from the beginning of existence, but live only in the here and now. Life exists only in the present.

Verse 15

In verse 15, Lao Tzu describes the ancient masters of Tai Chi who are to be examples for all Tai Chi students.

The ancient masters were subtle...

They did what their nature required them to do quietly and with such subtle moves that they did not attract attention. In other words, they were neither flashy nor demonstrative in their way of life. They taught others by their example, not by their words.

...mysterious...

Adults are very predictable because we have formed or been taught rigid ideas about what correct behaviour is. It appears mysterious to see an adult acting naturally, spontaneously, like a small child. Hence, the Tai Chi person, like the small child, is unpredictable.

...profound...

There was deep meaning in all that the ancient masters did, no matter how small and insignificant the task. For them, chopping wood and toting water were paths to understanding of the Tao because they were performed 100 per cent. I have found that the tasks of chopping wood and weeding the garden are two of the best activities for improving one's understanding of Tai Chi when done correctly.

...responsive.

The ancient masters were aware of what was occurring around them and responded to everything they encountered by establishing a harmony with all. Thus, the Tai Chi person must have the flexibility of mind, body and soul that is required to adapt and adjust to every new situation.

The depth of their knowledge is unfathomable.
Because it is unfathomable,
All we can do is describe their appearance.

Like the Tao and like Tai Chi, the Tai Chi person cannot be understood with the mind. He cannot be described in words. No one can tell you what the Tao is. No one can tell you what Tai Chi is. We can only describe the actions and the principles upon which they move. Thus, we can only describe how the Tai Chi person lives his life.

Watchful, like men crossing a winter stream.

The Tai Chi person lives every second of his life as if he were walking on stones across a winter stream. One slip of the foot and he falls into the freezing water. He is concentrated on his balance while at the same time feeling the surface of the stone and the firmness of his foothold. Such awareness is the essence of Tai Chi.

People who have lived through experiences of great danger often comment upon how alive they felt at the moment. Why do people climb mountains, jump out of airplanes, etc? When the mountain-climber hangs onto a cliff edge by his fingertips with death waiting if he makes a single mistake, every nerve in his body, every minute particle is focused 100 per cent on this second of life. There is only the here and now as every aspect of his being unites with his will in order to aid his progress. His eyes are aware of every crack in the surface of the rock, his fingertips become as sensitive as those of a brain surgeon as they feel for every possible handhold, his feet are continuously adjusting his balance, the skin is aware of every minute shift of the wind or drop in temperature. For him, time stands still. This second of life is all that exists.

Ask the mountain-climber why he does this dangerous activity and he will tell you that it is because he never feels so alive as when he's hanging on the cliff. We have all had experiences in our lives when we have felt such heightened awareness. What Tai Chi does is make such awareness fill every second of our lives. The Tai Chi person must watch every move lest he harm another. He must watch every word lest he destroys the harmony between himself and another. He must be extremely sensitive to the feelings of others and aware of their moods so that he is prepared to adjust instantly to any situation, offering aid, or yielding silently.

Alert, like men aware of danger.

In oriental philosophy, the warrior is often a symbol of mystical awareness. Every second of the Tai Chi person's life is like the Samurai warrior in a sword duel with another Samurai. The two Samurai stand facing each other, watching each other's every movement, all the senses alert. They can hear the people beginning to gather, the murmur of the crowd, the piece of paper blowing across the field, the dog barking, the wind blowing through the leaves of a tree, but are still focused with all their concentration upon the opponent.

The same type of concentration can be found in mothers. They can be engrossed in what they are doing but still be aware of the little child playing in the corner, and ready to respond immediately at the first hint of danger. Every second of the Tai Chi person's life is spent in such awareness. He must be totally concentrated on what he is doing but, at the same time, aware of everything happening around him.

Courteous, like visiting guests.

The worst that can happen to those who seek Oneness with all is separation and conflict. Separation and conflict are loss of Oneness and harmony. Thus, the Tai Chi person goes through life assuming the role of a visiting guest. He seeks neither to impose nor give offence.

Yielding, like ice about to melt.

Snow, when melting, loses its whiteness. It becomes transparent on the outer edges. One touch of the finger and it is gone. In Tai Chi, whether in self-defence or in everyday life, as soon as you meet something hard, like another person's opinion, or when you sense antagonism and feel its pressure, you yield instantly, you disappear in order to avoid conflict.

Simple, like uncarved blocks of wood.

All we need in order to survive is a place to sleep and food to eat. Everything else in life is extra. But we make our lives complicated and then become confused when we cannot untangle it. Be uncomplicated. Accept things as they are without building elaborate theories or seeking hidden motives. Why should you fear the motives of others? The Tai Chi person has nothing to lose.

Hollow, like caves.

The Tai Chi person must empty himself of goals, purpose, ambition, and hard, set ideas. He must rid himself of the ego. When such emptiness is obtained, all things can find refuge within him.

Opaque, like muddy pools.

The Tai Chi person is difficult for the world to understand. He follows no ordered pattern of behaviour. His actions are not motivated by ambition or desire for possession but arise spontaneously from the free flow of his nature. A world motivated by selfishness and greed will not be able to understand such a person.

Who can wait quietly while the mud settles?

Who can remain still in the midst of activity and wait until all aspects of a given situation can be seen clearly? Who has such patience? This capacity for patience is the essence of Tai Chi self-defence and of the Tai Chi life. It is the ability to wait for the moment of action and then to move with your total strength, willpower, mind, soul, and body.

Patience is a very rare commodity in our Western way of life. We Westerners try to force circumstances to be the way we want them to be, because we do not have the patience to wait for the correct conditions before we act. Often, when governments are faced with demands for action concerning poverty, resource-depletion, etc., they commence programmes that often result in making the problem worse. The patience to examine all the aspects of a problem and all the ramifications of the proposed answer is lacking.

This cultural difference between East and West often causes difficulties. American businessmen who are in a hurry to get things done are often upset by their Japanese business associates. To the American, the Japanese seem to be indecisive or even to be purposely dallying. But the Japanese are waiting for favourable circumstances for action. The Japanese know that trying to manipulate and force events can only lead to disaster. Because of this cultural difference, many oriental masters refuse to accept non-Asian students. They do not believe an American, for example, has the patience to learn their discipline.

Observers of the Tao do not seek fulfilment.

The Tai Chi person is seeking neither enlightenment nor anything else. To seek something is to have a goal, and to have a goal is a division between the goal itself, and the one trying to reach it. Thus, the One is destroyed. The river flows to the ocean not because it is seeking the ocean, but rather because that is its nature. Enlightenment is not our goal, but our destiny. We simply follow our nature and it takes us to our destiny without effort on our part.

Not seeking fulfilment, they are not swayed by desire for change.

Since the Tai Chi person is not seeking anything, he is content to let things take their natural course. The only change that will help anything is the change the individual makes within himself as he fills himself with compassion for his fellows and the world around him. Until human beings have this compassion and a feeling of Oneness, it does not matter what changes we make in government, economic systems, civil rights, etc., because without compassion and Oneness everything will remain based upon selfishness and ego. The Tai Chi person thus passes through life adapting and adjusting to all situations, all the while serving as an example of loving compassion and non-violence for all whom he meets.

Verse 16

Empty yourself of everything.

As long as you are full of yourself, of the ego, of hard, set ideas about the way things are, nothing can enter your consciousness without being distorted. When you are empty, all things can enter as they truly are. Nothing and no one is shut out.

Emptiness is an harmonious and tranquil state, and it is in harmony and tranquillity that the Tao is most fully revealed. When you are not distracted by the manifestations, it is possible to see the Oneness.

*The ten thousand things rise and fall while the Self
watches their return.*

The Tai Chi person remains unaffected, unswayed, unmoved as he watches the natural flow of the universe.

*They grow and flourish and then return to the source.
Returning to the source is stillness, which is the way of nature.*

All things come from the Tao and return to the Tao. The Tao is our source. Within the individual, the Tao is manifested in the Tan Tien, the point about 2 inches below the navel which is the Chi centre. The Tai Chi person keeps his mind focused on this point and, in so doing, attains stillness at his centre. The Tai Chi person becomes the still point in the ever-moving Tao. It is to him that the world can cling because he is always there, always secure, and where he is, is peace and rest.

Knowing constancy is insight.

If you can remain unmoved, if you can hold to your centre without losing your harmony and tranquillity, then you see clearly what is occurring around you.

Not knowing constancy leads to disaster.

When we are not rooted to our centre and cannot maintain our harmony, we cannot see clearly but, instead, see the world through the distorting mesh of our fears, prejudices, and separateness. Seeing falsely, we will react to the world from emotion rather than from compassion.

With an open mind, you will be openhearted.

If the mind is open, then there is nothing that cannot come into it. Many people are afraid of certain thoughts, of contemplating certain ideas. There is the fear that if these ideas were accepted, they could cause their lives to change in ways they cannot predict. Such people have a fear of the unknown. But, if you can remain unmoved, sure of your centre and your path, it does not matter what enters the mind. Because no matter how your life may be changed by new ideas, you know that your harmony and tranquillity will remain undisturbed in any situation. So, what is there to fear? And once you no longer fear ideas, you no longer fear the people who have them. Your heart can be open to anyone, no matter how radical his ideas, because you are sure of who and what you are.

Being openhearted, you will act royally.

When you are openhearted you can be impartial to all whom you meet. The communist and the capitalist, the rich man and the poor man, the atheist and the believer, the black radical and the white racist, the murderer and the saint; all are the same and all are to be welcomed with compassionate love by the openhearted person.

Being royal, you will attain the divine.

Knowing constancy, openheartedness, and openmindedness you will be like the Tao. The Tao accepts everything and everyone as its child. It has no preferences and makes no judgements, and thus is the example that guides the life of the Tai Chi person.

Being at one with the Tao is eternal.
And though the body dies, the Tao will never pass away.

When you are one with the Tao, you assume its characteristics;

its tranquillity, its compassion, and its eternity. These lines are the closest that Lao Tzu comes to speaking about life after death. Something must survive because the Tao is eternal, and you are part of the Tao. The Tao is a Oneness and could not exist without you.

Verse 19

Give up sainthood, renounce wisdom,
And it will be a hundred times better for everyone.

Tai Chi people are not seeking enlightenment. Enlightenment is the destination toward which human nature flows. It is the natural result of becoming one with ourselves and the universe around us. Hence, enlightenment is not something we seek, but rather, something we await to develop.

Further, the Tai Chi person is not concerned with being 'holy', at least not as that term is commonly understood. The label of sainthood is commonly attached to a person who has renounced evil and who has become one with goodness. But in Tai Chi there is no separation between good and evil. There are only relationships among things and people. Some relationships are harmonious and some violate the principles of the Tao, of Oneness. For example, there is nothing good or bad about a piece of lead. The piece of lead and I exist in harmony, neither harming the other. I can take the piece of lead and use it to make a shield in order to protect myself from X-rays. By so doing, I establish a new but still harmonious relationship between myself and the piece of lead. However, if someone takes the piece of lead, makes it into a bullet, and shoots it into my body, the lead and I no longer have a harmonious relationship. That does not mean that the piece of lead is evil. It simply means that pieces of lead do not belong inside human bodies.

It is not even possible to say that the person who shoots me is evil or that he did an evil thing. He is simply committing an act that violates the principles of the Tao and thus is heading for disaster. The Tai Chi person does not renounce the use of lead because it can kill people but, rather, seeks to establish a harmonious relationship with it.

In the same vein, a person who feeds me when I am hungry is not good. If he feeds me because it is his nature to help a starving man, then he had no choice. If his act did not come from his nature then he has some personal motive for helping me and does not deserve to be labelled 'good'.

Thus, the term 'holiness' in Tai Chi has nothing to do with good and evil; rather, it indicates that the person is 'whole', 'complete', that he has harmonised himself with all that exists, the good and the bad. To say that someone is a spiritual person, for example, means that he or she is imbalanced. What happened to the material? If the material aspect of life has been renounced, then the person is neither one with himself, nor one with the universe. The same holds true for the person labelled as materialistic.

Verse 22

Yield and overcome.

This is the basic teaching of Tai Chi and is a fundamental characteristic of the Tao. By yielding in the face of aggression, we take away the force of the aggression. For example, I am working in an office and a man enters who is obviously very upset and angry. He begins to yell at me. If I respond with harsh words in return, that only serves to increase his anger and prolongs our separateness and conflict. On the other hand, if I do not respond with anger, he will find it very difficult to maintain his anger and aggression. Arguing becomes a very tiring process if the other person does not argue back. Soon, the force of his anger will be spent and then the weakness of my compassion will be able to overcome his anger completely.

Naturally, this principle is an integral part of Tai Chi self-defence. The Tai Chi person always yields in the face of aggression. Strength must have something to make contact with or it turns into its opposite, weakness. Try punching the air with all your strength. At the end of the punch, you will be weak and off balance. When Yang goes too far, it changes into Yin. Thus, there are no attacks in Tai Chi, only responses. The Tai Chi person waits for the attack and then yields so that the strike passes by harmlessly. When the attacker meets no resistance, he loses his strength and balance and that is when the Tai Chi person responds with a strike powered by Chi or with a hold.

Bend and be straight...

The Tai Chi person is moving straight toward his own nature, towards Oneness with the Tao. Nothing can divert him from his path, but it is a winding, curving path that he follows, a path that twists and turns around obstacles. By yielding, bending, adjusting, and adapting, he moves straight toward his destiny.

Empty and be full...

Empty yourself of hard, set ideas about the way the universe is. Empty yourself of ego and ambition. Empty yourself of fear. When you are empty, all of existence comes rushing in to fill the vacuum. All people and all things find a refuge in your emptiness.

Have little and gain;
Have much and be confused.

The more possessions you have, the more things you are attached to, the less freedom you will have because of the energy and time that is required to protect them. The people with the least freedom in the world are prisoners and the wealthy. The prisoner's freedom is lost because of his crimes. The wealthy man's freedom is lost because of his possessions. Both the prisoner and the wealthy man live behind high walls with spotlights, wire, and guards. The rich can afford fantastic amusements in their beautiful prisons, but they remain prisons nonetheless. For everything that you are attached to, for everything you fear to lose, some freedom must be surrendered.

Most people's houses are filled with possessions to which they are very attached and, therefore, they must lock their houses whenever they leave. As a result, they are chained to the key. They have lost the freedom simply to leave without worry. If someone leaves for a vacation and then cannot remember if he locked his house, his entire vacation will be ruined and filled with anxiety.

The answer to the problem of possessions is to own nothing which if stolen would bother you. Then you need never worry about locking your house. The more valued possessions you have, the more time, energy, and money you must spend guarding them. Have things with you for your use, but do not be attached to them. This must be the way of the Tai Chi person because Tai Chi is a path that runs toward absolute freedom.

In poorer, rural areas, it is still possible to find whole communities and isolated farms where people do not lock their houses. When people are away, whether for half an hour or for several days, a message is left on the door informing everyone of the time they left, the time they expect to return, and inviting the visitor to make himself comfortable until they do.

Strangers passing through come into the house, make a fire, and cook a meal. The visitor leaves a message of his own on the door before he goes to sleep informing the owners that he is there in case they come home during the night. The next morning, the visitor washes the dirty dishes, prepares wood in the fireplace, and leaves a note on the door thanking the owners for their hospitality. Such a situation is possible because these poor, rural people have, in their own eyes, little worth stealing. Thus they can afford to be hospitable.

Therefore wise men embrace the one
And set an example to all.

Tai Chi is not something that can be learned from books and lectures. It is something that must be experienced. The student learns by following the example of the Tai Chi teacher and imitating his movements as closely as possible. In so doing, the student must trust that the Tai Chi teacher is imitating the movements of the Tao or, in other words, 'embracing the one'. If such trust does not exist, the student should seek another teacher.

Not putting on a display,
They shine forth.

The Tai Chi person who has reached Oneness has no need for show. In fact, it is just the opposite. The Tai Chi person disappears as he blends into the background that is the Tao. In Tai Chi there are no great gurus. An ostentatious show is a sure sign that the Tai Chi person has lost his way. Fame is to be avoided. Anyone who is centred in harmony and tranquillity will, in this greatly disturbed world of ours, be recognised. This recognition will come from the heart and not from the consciousness of others. People will be attracted to him without realising that he is in any way special and without even realising how much they depend upon him in times of trouble. The Tai Chi person is like the guest at a party who gave the party a special flavour with his warmth and humour, but whose face and name no one can remember the next day.

Not justifying themselves,
They are distinguished.

Without excuses, without ambition, the Tai Chi person does that which flows from his nature and, in so doing, accomplishes everything that needs to be done.

Not boasting,
They receive recognition.
Not bragging,

They never falter.

The Tai Chi person does not boast about what he will do because that is in the future, and because his actions flow spontaneously from his nature. Thus, he does not know what he will do in the future. He does not brag about what he has accomplished because that is the past and the Tai Chi person lives only in the here and now.

They do not quarrel,
So no one quarrels with them.

If you do not compete with others, then no one can compete with you. Competition, no matter what the circumstances, is separation. If somebody wins, somebody else must lose. What will your winning do to this other person? How can you take pleasure in someone losing?

When I was in high school, I played the tuba in the school band. I had a loving family, good grades, and good friends. There were five other tuba-players in the band and one of them was a boy who came from a poor family situation, had bad grades, and few, if any, friends. The only thing that he had was his ability to play the tuba fairly well. One day the band director told us that we all had to play some music to see which one of us would be first tuba. We played and I was the winner. By winning the contest, I took away the one thing the other boy had. He began crying and I told the band director that I did not want to be first tuba. The band director refused to allow me to surrender first place. Later, the other boy quit the band. I vowed then that I would never compete with anyone again. It was my first Tai Chi lesson and I have never forgotten it.

Quarrelling is a form of competition. The Tai Chi person does not quarrel because he has nothing to defend. He has no set ideas and he does not require acceptance of his behaviour or of his beliefs. But he realises that most people do have ingrained ideas and views of the world and to present challenges to those ideas and views causes fear and antagonism. Therefore the Tai Chi person does not try to change the thinking or behaviour of another, and the basis for quarrelling is removed.

Therefore the ancients say, 'Yield and overcome.'
Is that an empty saying?

Not to the student of Tai Chi: it is the essence of Tai Chi and the Tai Chi way of life.

Be really whole,
And all things will come to you.

When you are one with yourself, when you have entered into the flow of the universe, then all things will be attracted to you, because in you they will find harmony and peace.

Verse 24

He who stands on tiptoe is not steady.
He who strides cannot maintain the pace.

Extremes cannot be maintained. Go too far and you get the opposite of what you seek. In Tai Chi, we never rise up on our toes because there is no balance there. The body is extended too far. Dancers who come to learn Tai Chi often have difficulties in adjusting to our philosophy of balance. A dancer can stand on his toes and twirl. But, as Tai Chi is also a system of self-defence, the Tai Chi person should never be in a position where he cannot withstand a blow or a push without losing his balance. In life, you must never go to extremes where the blows that life deals will make you lose your centredness.

He who makes a show is not enlightened.

Whenever you make a show, you attract attention to yourself and that is dangerous to your development as a Tai Chi person. In Tai Chi, we blend in with the world rather than stand out. Pass through life unnoticed and no one will interfere with your journey.

He who is self-righteous is not respected.

If you do not respect the beliefs, ideas, and ways of others you will not be respected in your turn. The Tai Chi person does not interfere with the lives of others and does not judge their journey through life.

He who boasts achieves nothing.

The purpose of boasting is to attract attention or some other form of reward for your actions. There is no reward for the Tai Chi person except the peace and harmony at the centre of his existence.

He who brags will not endure.

Opposites are inseparably connected. Thus, sooner or later, success must be followed by failure. To brag is not to understand the nature of things.

According to followers of the Tao,
'These are extra food and unnecessary luggage'.
They do not bring happiness.
Therefore followers of the Tao avoid them.

Anyone who has travelled very far knows that you do not want to carry unnecessary baggage. Boasting, self-righteousness, and ostentation are all unnecessary encumbrances for a journey to the Tao and to yourself. They will only slow you down and the Tai Chi person avoids them.

Verse 25

Something mysteriously formed.
Born before heaven and earth.

Tai Chi philosophy makes no claim to intellectual knowledge. Tai Chi is concerned only with this second in your life and how you are living it. There is no figure in Tai Chi like the French philosopher René Descartes, who sat in his room and tried to know the universe with his mind. Such an approach would seem the height of foolishness to a Tai Chi person. Knowledge only comes through experience. The problem for Tai Chi is that words cannot describe the knowledge that comes from experience. Such knowledge must be experienced by each individual if he is also to have that knowledge. So throughout The Tao Te Ching Lao Tzu is at a loss for words as he tries to describe that which cannot be described. This is also the problem for the Tai Chi teacher. The teacher could talk for hours about Tai Chi and never really be able to tell the student what it is. All that Lao Tzu and the Tai Chi teacher can do is try to give you glimpses of what the Tao and Tai Chi are.

So, when the student asks what the Tao is, I say, 'I do not know'. It is 'something' (I do not know what) 'mysteriously formed' (I do not know how), 'born before heaven and earth' (it is the Mother of all that is).

In the silence and the void...

From the silence and the Void, the Tao arose. Hence, silence and emptiness are the nature of all that exists. It is this silent and empty nature that Tai Chi helps the student to discover within himself by means of the silent and empty movements that are its teaching.

Standing alone and unchanging...

Though the universe is continuous change, the principles which govern this change remain ever the same. Thus, the Tai Chi movements are continuous as they flow from Yin to Yang and back, but the principles that govern their flow are unchanging. The Tai Chi student continuously moves through life adjusting, changing and adapting, but the principles of non-violence, harmony, and love that govern his movements are unchanging.

The Tai Chi student, like the Tao, stands alone. There is nothing he can hold to except his own centre. By holding to his centre, remaining unmoved, he becomes the centre of the universe and a great source of strength for all of the people around him. People will know that, no matter what catastrophes occur, there will always be one point in the universe that remains tranquil and full of peace: the Tai Chi person is that point. Tai Chi is called the 'unmoving movement' because, although the Tai Chi person is continuously moving, he remains unmoved at his centre.

I do not know its name.
Call it Tao.

Lao Tzu is saying that he does not know what the force is that governs the universe, or rather, that he does not know it in intellectual terms. He simply knows that it is there and that it is the 'Way'.

Man follows the earth.
Earth follows heaven.
Heaven follows the Tao.
Tao follows what is natural.

The Tao is pure process, pure movement, that flows spontaneously in accordance with certain principles. It is the Great Mother of all that exists. Heaven (Yang, the male) follows the Tao (Yin, the female). Earth (Yin) follows heaven (Yang). Human beings follow earth (Yin). Thus, human beings should follow the way of Yin Chi (that is, non-violence, compassion, intuitive knowledge, yielding, weakness, flexibility, softness, etc.). Tai Chi is the way of Yin Chi, the way of the female. That is why many more women than men are attracted to Tai Chi and the average Tai Chi school has between 60 and 80 per cent women students. Our societies teach men that strength and aggression are masculine traits. Such ideas have no place in Tai Chi and anyone holding such ideas will have a very difficult time learning Tai Chi. In Tai Chi, the role of the male is that of a compassionate loving father who accepts the whole world as his child. He is the provider for those in need and the defender of the helpless. He relies upon the union of his will with his Chi, rather than upon muscular strength to fulfil his masculinity. He is not offended if he is held in low esteem by other men because he knows who and what he is and where he is going.

Verse 26

The heavy is the root of the light...

Depth of soul and understanding, fullness of compassion, and weight of character are the qualities that root you to your path. Flitting around from one thing to the next, unable to find a centre, will keep you from ever making any kind of progress. I have students who spend one weekend at the Buddhist Meditation Retreat, the next weekend at the conference for dream analysis, and the third weekend practising yoga somewhere. This way of going through life keeps them from becoming rooted to a path and from having to look deeply within themselves.

The still is the master of unrest.

If the student remains still and fixed within himself, he will be able to see clearly what is happening around him and to feel what it is that his nature requires of him in any given situation. If he is unsettled, swinging violently from one emotion to the next, it will be very difficult for him to control himself and the situation around him. It is the same in Tai Chi self-defence. As long as the Tai Chi person remains in his centre, rooted to the ground, and in a position of balance, he can control every part of his body. But if he loses his balance and surrenders his control, the other person seizes it. It is true of self-defence and it is true of life.

Therefore the sage, travelling all day,
Does not lose sight of his baggage.

On your journey to the Tao, do not lose sight of that which is important: tranquillity, harmony, silence, compassion, and emptiness. These are the essentials you will need to reach your true destiny.

To be light is to lose one's root.
To be restless is to lose one's control.

It is impossible to practise Tai Chi when angry or when some other unsettling emotion is going on inside. Such emotions take the student away from his centre. He will be unable to find his balance and unable to unite his mind and body. Thus at the beginning of each Tai Chi class the first thirty minutes should be spent in relaxing, calming exercises to give the student a chance to shed the emotions and anxieties he has gathered during the day.

Verse 27

A good walker leaves no tracks...

He leaves no tracks because he is one with the ground that he is passing over. The Tai Chi person passes through life without leaving disturbance in his wake. He passes unseen and unheard, blending in with the world around him.

A good speaker makes no slips...

He is one with everything he is saying because everything he says comes from his heart. He is sparing with his words and does not speak in order to hear his own voice or simply to attract attention to himself.

A good reckoner needs no tally.

He is not separated from that which his mind is considering. Every object that he touches, every idea that he contemplates, every person that he meets is but an extension of himself.

Therefore the sage takes care of all men
And abandons no one.
He takes care of all things
And abandons nothing.

The Tao is a totality composed of all things and all people. If even one piece is missing the totality is lost and the Tao is no more. Everything is important to everything else. The Tai Chi person renounces nothing and no one but, instead, helps all people and all things to reach a state of harmony. To the Tao and to the Tai Chi person, there is no such thing as a useless object or a worthless person. No matter how worthless or base a person may seem, the harmony of the universe and of myself depends upon him. So I cannot find Oneness and peace unless you also find them. The Tao that I am moving towards will never be there unless you are with me. I must help you in every way I can. This is called 'following the light of understanding'. This is the only true enlightenment: to establish harmony between yourself and all whom you meet. If everyone in the universe existed in harmony and peace with each other but you were not part of this harmony, then the Oneness would be lost for all of us. How can I abandon you? Either we all go together or no one goes. Hence, it is like Tai Chi. The class must be one with each other for the beauty and the harmony of the movements to emerge. If just one student is not focused, or is off balance, or has the wrong timing, the harmony of the whole is lost. Every student depends on every other student. Each must adjust and adapt to the others. Either all the class does Tai Chi, or no one does.

What is a good man?
A teacher of a bad man.
What is a bad man?
A good man's charge.

These lines are a statement of the responsibilities the student assumes when he begins the Tai Chi journey. Through the insights of Tai Chi, the student realises that the entire universe is depending upon him. Harmony will be lost to the universe as long as he does not become one with his nature and as long as he does not follow that nature to where it takes him. He, alone, is responsible for the peace and tranquillity of the Tao. This means that where there is disharmony anywhere in the universe, it is his fault. If there is someone starving, if there is war, if someone is homeless, if someone is racially oppressed, if nature is polluted, if a child is abused, if someone is sick, it is the Tai Chi person's fault. If he had done what his nature requires of him, only harmony would reign throughout the Tao. But this realisation does not come from a logical analysis of life, nor does Tai Chi teach it: it gradually develops from within the Tai Chi student himself as he journeys ever nearer the Oneness with his own nature.

Tai Chi's method for overcoming the disharmony of the world is by example. Tai Chi is taught by example and the harmonious life is taught by example. The Tai Chi teacher demonstrates the Tai Chi movements to his students. The Tai Chi person teaches the world the harmonious life by demonstrating it. As in Tai Chi, exhortations and lectures will do no good.

If the teacher is not respected,
And the student not cared for,
Confusion will arise, however clever one is.

When a student joins a Tai Chi school, he enters a pact with the teacher. The student must give the teacher his respect, his attention, and his loyalty. In exchange, the teacher must give the student love and understanding. The teacher must do everything he can to aid the student in his journey to his nature. If either the student or the teacher fails to fulfil his part of the pact, the student–teacher relationship should be terminated and the student should find another teacher. Otherwise the whole school will suffer.

I have seen schools where the teacher is concerned only with teaching the students the Tai Chi movements and takes no interest in their lives. He does not know their joys, hopes, and fears, and has no idea whether they are being given what they need. In other words, the relationship is one of a businessman and his customers.

On the other hand, I have seen schools where some of the students show disrespect to the teacher by not paying him on time, by being frequently late to class, and by not informing the teacher when a class must be missed. But the worst disrespect is from the student who disagrees with his teacher's behaviour or teaching and does not quit the school, but stays and complains to the other students. Such a situation can only harm the school.

This is the crux of mystery.

The bond of respect for the teacher and love for the student is essential for the learning of Tai Chi. Why this is so is a mystery, but it is so.

Verse 28

Know the strength of man,
But keep a woman's care!

A woman does not have the same muscular strength as a man and cannot force her way through life. She must be more careful than the male in avoiding violent situations. Hence the female is a symbol of Tai Chi. Lao Tzu is saying that you should understand the Yang, how strength, force, and aggression are used, what brings them into play, etc., but you should hold to the Yin, to non-violence, softness, gentleness, compassion, etc.

Be the stream of the universe!
Being the stream of the universe,
Ever true and unswerving,
Become as a little child once more.

By becoming one with the universe, the Tai Chi person is the universe, ever true and unswerving in his following of the principles of the Tao. This development is possible because the Tai Chi person has the characteristics of a small child.

The infant is a symbol of the Tao and of Tai Chi. The infant has no preconceived plans, but simply acts as he feels. This spontaneity of feeling and behaviour keeps life interesting to the infant. Everything and everyone he meets is unique, fresh, and new. We adults have already categorised everything. If I see a rock, I see it as like all other rocks. It is hard and does not do very much. I have seen thousands of rocks and they are all pretty much the same to me. But my son can pick up a rock and carry it all the way back home as we walk through the forest, just for the feel of its weight and the smoothness of its surface. He experiences the uniqueness of this particular rock and becomes one with it. An interesting thing, this rock.

But it is not just the rock that is interesting to my son. He is fascinated with everything he comes in contact with: a bottle cap, a worm, a dead frog, a button, etc. While we walk along, I am in my rational mind thinking about this or that personal problem, or remembering something from the past, or daydreaming about the future. But my son is here and now. He is experiencing life. For him, the world is an endlessly fascinating and magical place where nothing is to be missed. He experiences the uniqueness of all things while, to me, a rock is just a rock and a button is just a button.

My little boy is the same with people as he is with things. He ignores the categorisations of adulthood and, as a result, can relate to each person as an individual. Age, race, nationality, religion, and sex mean nothing to him. He is the same to all whom he meets. No matter who it is, he finds that place within them where he can laugh and play and sing. In other words, he finds their uniqueness.

We adults, on the other hand, have categorised people in the same way that we have categorised everything else. Categorising is what the mind does and the mind is where adults spend their lives. The tragedy is that in the process of categorisation, the uniqueness of the individual is lost. As soon as we meet someone, we categorise them by sex, age, nationality, etc., and each category carries with it a bundle of definitions. She is like this because she is a woman. She is like that because she is over sixty. The process of defining continues until, by the time we get through all of the categories, the person has lost the uniqueness of her being and her existence. We do not see the fascinating details of her life as a unique occurrence in the Tao. We begin to feel cut off from others and alienated from society. This state of affairs can be halted by becoming 'as a little child once more'. In other words, live in the heart rather than in the mind.

A further characteristic of the infant that is important for the Tai Chi person is the fact that while the infant's body is weak, he has tremendous strength and willpower within himself. Every mother knows that a child can scream for hours and not become hoarse and how he can cling to a toy or sweet with all his being.

The child has flexibility in the body, in the mind, and in the soul. He has not yet been moulded into a certain view of life, and so he can adapt to almost any situation. The child is at home anywhere. The child has no extra baggage because he lives in the here and now.

Know the white,
But keep the black!

White is Yang. It is the colour of glory and death. Thus, in the Orient, white is the colour worn at funerals. Black is the colour of life, the female, humility, mystery, and invisibility. In Japanese Noh plays, the people who change the scenery wear black. The acting continues as these people come onto the stage to prepare for the next scene. This can be very distracting to the Western viewer, but not to the Japanese. To the Japanese viewer, the people in black are invisible.

Karate, judo, and other aggressive martial arts practitioners wear white, because these disciplines originated and developed within the Samurai or warrior caste of Japan. The warrior must be fearless and prepared for death at any second. So white is worn by adherents of these disciplines to demonstrate their readiness to meet death.

In Tai Chi, we wear black. We are not warriors but, instead, followers of the female aspect of life. In my own school, I require the wearing of black. This accomplishes two things: (1) it helps to instil the traditional spirit of Tai Chi so that the student sees that what he is doing is not just a pastime or entertainment, and (2) it helps the student to disappear into the Oneness of the group.

The uniformity of dress, or at least of colour, does not in any way detract from the individuality of the student. Tai Chi must be practised alone so that the student can move at his own tempo and experience his own Chi. When alone, it does not matter what clothes the student wears, or at what speed he does the moves, because he is alone and getting to know himself. But Tai Chi must also be practised in a group. For that reason, I do not teach people in private lessons. Tai Chi helps the student become one with himself and one with others. Practising alone takes care of the first part and learning with a group teaches him to be one with others. When the student is in the class he, like everyone else, must adjust his speed to the others. He must disappear into the class just as he must disappear into the Tao. The wearing of black aids this process. I should not look in the door and see Bill in his blue T-shirt, Joan in her red halter-top, and Henry in his yellow jogging suit. I should look in the door and simply see Tai Chi; I should see a Oneness where each individual has disappeared into the whole.

Some students have difficulty in accepting this approach. In the West, the grasping for individuality and uniqueness has gone to such lengths that people can no longer co-operate, as each seeks his own personal fulfilment. They do not understand that the fullest development of the individual can only come through the development of humanity as a whole. The right arm has unique abilities, but if it does not co-operate with the rest of the body, it is a useless appendage.

Be an example to the world!

On his journey toward Oneness with himself and others, the Tai Chi person serves as an example to all he comes into contact with.

Know honour,
Yet keep humility.

People seek honour, glory, and high status out of a desire to feel important. The Tai Chi person must understand this and avoid coming between people and their desires in order to avoid conflict. As for himself, he accepts humility as a way of life and being unimportant as an asset.

Be the valley of the universe!

Everything grows and is nourished in the fertility of the valley. The Tai Chi person becomes the valley of the universe by helping everything and everyone to grow towards their destiny, and by nourishing them with the compassion that fills his being.

Return to the state of the uncarved block.
When the block is carved, it becomes useful.

A block of wood is fairly useless until it is carved into a shape that fulfils some desired function. Our societies carve people into complicated shapes so that we can be used to fulfil the roles that have been socially formed for us. Only after this shaping can we be manipulated. The discipline of Tai Chi helps the student to return to the simple, natural state of existence that he had before the complex, fixed ideas of his society were forced upon him. When such simplicity is attained, he can no longer be manipulated by others. He is useless in other people's efforts to achieve fame and material gain.

Verse 29

Do you think you can take over the universe and improve it?
I do not believe it can be done.

That is exactly what societies believe. Only human beings seek to interfere with nature, to change it according to our own desires. Such interference can only lead to disaster. The universe is a Oneness and when there is no interference with its principles, everything works in harmony. There is no need to repair it or to try and improve it. Interference can only upset the balance of things. Because of our separation from nature, we see it as something plastic that we can mould and shape as we wish. The creation of deserts, the destruction of rain-forests, the destruction of the ozone layer, the extinction of animal species, the depletion of the water resources, etc. are all results of this egotistical assumption. And in the process of all this destruction we are destroying ourselves because, whether we realise it or not, we and nature are one.

The universe is sacred.
You cannot improve it.
If you try to change it, you will ruin it.
If you try to hold it, you will lose it.

By sacred, Lao Tzu means that the universe is complete. Nothing is missing. So leave it alone and harmonise yourself to it. He goes on to say that everything must change, so hold onto nothing but your own centre.

Verse 30

Whenever you advise a ruler in the way of Tao,
Counsel him not to use force to conquer the universe.
For this would only cause resistance.

Force cannot be used against people in order to get them to do something. To force people is violence to the human soul. The use of force causes resentment and resistance. This is true whether in a personal argument or in armed conflict between nations. History is full of the failures that result from the use of force. The Irish have resisted the English for 800 years, for example. Force may work for the moment, it may even work for hundreds of years, but in the end it must fail. This lesson would seem to be obvious, but humanity has not yet learned it.

Understanding the uselessness of force is why the Tai Chi person avoids conflict as much as possible. He knows that even if he fights and wins, the loser's resentment will remain and fester, and widen further the rift between them.

Thorn bushes spring up wherever the army has passed.
Lean years follow in the wake of a great war.

Conflict and strife always leave destruction in their wake. Harmonious relationships are hard to establish where resentment and anger have held sway.

Just do what needs to be done.

The Tai Chi person avoids conflict and the use of self-defence at almost any cost, but there may come a time when he must defend himself to preserve his life and health, or the life and health of another. In such a case, the Tai Chi person must be prepared to do what he must. When the Oneness and harmony have been lost, the first tactic of Tai Chi is to apologise for whatever offence you might have caused. If an apology does not suffice and the other insists on continuing the conflict, then run away. If running away is not possible, Tai Chi teaches avoidance and evasion techniques that can be used to tire out the aggressor until his anger has dissipated. As a last resort, when all else fails, the Tai Chi person puts the aggressor into a disabling hold or uses a temporarily disabling strike. The Tai Chi student does only that which he has to do and because of that, does not have to worry if his actions are right or wrong.

Achieve results,
But never glory in them.
Achieve results,
But never boast.
Achieve results,
But never be proud.

The river that flows by the city achieves many varied results. It cleans our clothes, quenches our thirst, waters our crops, and makes our flowers bloom. These achievements are a result of the nature of water. Such are the achievements of the Tai Chi person also.

Achieve results,
Because this is the natural way.

Because you are a living being, you must act. Results are inevitable. As long as your actions arise spontaneously from your nature, you do not have to be concerned with the results.

Achieve results,
But not through violence.

Violence is separation from others and from yourself. You can never realise the fullest development of your own nature in separation from the Oneness.

Force is followed by loss of strength.
This is not the way of Tao.
That which goes against the Tao
Comes to an early end.

The use of force violates the principles of the Tao and Tai Chi never uses it. Even the best-trained fighters cannot fight for more than five minutes at a stretch without becoming exhausted.

The muscles have only a certain amount of strength, but the supply of Chi is unlimited. Thus, it is upon the Chi that the Tai Chi person relies.

Verse 31

Good weapons are instruments of fear; all creatures hate them.
Therefore followers of the Tao never use them.
The wise man prefers the left.
The man of war prefers the right.

If you are one with the Tao, there will be no conflicts and no need for weapons. People who are one with the Tao never use weapons. The wise person, he who understands the principles of the universe and who follows them, follows the left (Yin, non-aggression, non-violence, compassion, etc.). He who does not have this understanding follows the right (Yang, strength, force, violence, etc.).

Weapons are instruments of fear; they are not a wise man's tools.
He uses them only when he has no choice.

To repeat, if you are one with the Tao, there will be no need for weapons. However, in your journey to the Tao there might be a time when you have lost the Oneness and, at such times, weapons may be needed. Thus, Tai Chi also trains with weapons when the student has been practising for a long period of time. The Tai Chi Chuan, the 108 movements that are the basic discipline of Tai Chi, teaches the student to be one with himself and one with other people. The result is that every part of his body becomes an extension of the student's Chi so that it does exactly what he wills it to do. Training with weapons teaches the student to become one with inanimate objects so that everything he touches becomes an extension of himself. His Chi flows through the weapon and it becomes as much a part of him as his own arm. When the student can do that with a weapon, he can do it with the knife with which he cuts the tomato, with his piano, and so on.

The most important weapon studied in Tai Chi is the rattan staff.

It is the ideal weapon for Tai Chi because it is flexible and does not do much damage when it strikes. In ancient China, peasants were not allowed to have weapons but everyone had a rattan staff to aid walking on steep mountain paths and for carrying bundles. It is, therefore, the weapon of the humble. But let me reiterate that neither Tai Chi self-defence, nor the Tai Chi rattan staff can be learned in a traditional school until the student has studied for several years. If the student is not rooted in non-violence and compassion when he comes to Tai Chi, either he will be after several years of Tai Chi practice, or he will have left.

Peace and quiet are dear to his heart,
And victory no cause for rejoicing.

Peace and quiet are dear to the heart of the Tai Chi person because these are necessary conditions for the fullest contact with his nature and clarity of insight. Conflict and competition represent a loss of these conditions, and even a victory does not compensate for the subsequent loss of harmony. To rejoice in victory even in a harmless game means that you delight in someone's defeat. If you rejoice in a military victory, it means that you rejoice in killing. It may be necessary at some point for the Tai Chi person successfully to defend himself, but even this victory is a defeat for someone moving towards Oneness with all people. All conflict is separation and there is no way that you can fulfil yourself or find your uniqueness in separation from others.

> *On happy occasions precedence is given to the left,*
> *On sad occasions to the right.*
> *In the army the general stands on the left,*
> *The commander-in-chief on the right.*
> *This means that war is conducted like a funeral.*
> *When many people are being killed,*
> *They should be mourned in heartfelt sorrow.*
> *That is why victory must be observed like a funeral.*

The commander-in-chief is the one who makes the decision to go to war. Therefore, he stands on the right, the Yang side. The general simply follows the orders of the commander-in-chief and stands on the left, the Yin side. At a funeral, the honoured position is on the right but on happy occasions it is on the left. Joy comes from the Yin (non-violence, compassion, gentleness, etc.). Sadness comes from the Yang (aggression, anger, etc.). War and conflict are times of sadness and the fact of victory does not erase the pain and death that were caused. Even victory gives no cause for rejoicing. You should only enter into conflict when you have absolutely no other choice. If such a situation occurs, it is because you, the Tai Chi person, have failed to maintain your Oneness with others. When victory comes to you, it must be accepted with humility and compassion for the defeated. Humility and compassion will lessen the resentment that inevitably develops after defeat.

If nations could act upon this understanding of victory as an occasion for sadness, the history of the world would be changed. The Second World War was the direct result of the humiliations that the Germans were forced to suffer at the hands of the victors in the First World War. At the end of the Second World War, the Germans were again punished and humiliated with the division of their country. That division is one of the conditions that may lead to a third world war. What a different world it would be if we had convinced the Germans of our deep sadness over the losses they, as well as we, had suffered. Instead, we treat the defeated as if the conflict were totally their fault and, as a result, do not learn from our own mistakes.

Victory should be a time of mourning and of self-examination. Any conflict is a failure to maintain Oneness and harmony. It takes two to have a conflict, and every conflict is a defeat even to the victor. The victor must look within himself to see how he failed to establish a Oneness with himself and the opponent.

Verse 32

The Tao is forever undefined.

Like Tai Chi, the Tao cannot be understood with the mind and it cannot be explained in words. It must be experienced.

Small though it is in the unformed state, it cannot be grasped.

In its smallest manifestation, the Tao is the Tan Tien, the Chi centre in each individual. Even in this infinitely small aspect, it cannot be grasped with the intellect.

If kings and lords could harness it,
The ten thousand things would naturally obey.

If governments understood the principles of the Tao, there would be no war and no starvation, because governments could arrange their economies and laws to be in harmony with nature and with the principles that guide all things. Such economies and laws would not be based upon wishes, desires and competition, but upon knowledge, co-operation and a clear insight of how things really are. For example, some nations have laws against inter-racial marriage. Such laws demonstrate a lack of understanding of human love. People fall in love with each other despite racial differences. No law can change that, and therefore any such law is doomed to failure.

A nation that could attune itself to the principles of Tai Chi would seem to be 'obeyed' by the universe. The government would be like the boatman who lives according to the principles of the river. He sails safely where he will because he knows how to use the currents and how to set the sails in order to take advantage of the wind. He is the master of the river and the river aids him in all that he does, because he is one with the nature of the river and flows with it.

If nations could achieve harmony with the Tao, human development on this planet would be greatly enhanced. By ridding themselves of greed and the ambition to be 'the best', the environment would be protected. By adhering to non-aggression and humility in dealing with others, wars would be no more. By developing a sense of compassion for all life, starvation would disappear. Governments are simply a reflection of their citizens. If the citizens do not adhere to such principles in dealing with each other, how can their governments? The future of our world will be decided by our individual behaviour in personal relationships. The harmony of the entire universe depends upon you and me. The Tai Chi person realises this and by basing his own life upon these principles he helps his own nation move toward harmony. As his nation moves towards realisation of these principles, it helps the entire world move towards harmony. In other words, the Tai Chi person serves as a model for his nation and his nation serves as a model for the world.

Heaven and earth would come together
And gentle rain fall.

In a nation whose people were attuned to the Tao, everything would be allowed to move towards its natural development. Yin and

Yang, the male and the female, would come together in harmony and bring forth the new.

Men would need no more instruction and all things would take their course.

Everything would be one with its own nature and would move towards its own destiny. In such a world there would be no more need for Tai Chi teachers.

Once the whole is divided, the parts need names.

As long as things are united in a Oneness, there is no need for names. Names are labels that are attached to separate entities in order to point out their differences. Only when the Oneness is lost does the need for names and categories arise. That is why I do not like to teach my students the names of each of the 108 moves in the Tai Chi Chuan. I do not want them thinking in terms of 108 separate movements. In Tai Chi, there is only one move. When the students perceive this unity, they are able to flow between the movements without stopping and thus their movements are more fluid and harmonious. When a student asks me the name of a movement, I tell him, but I do not go out of my way to teach the name.

Once the Oneness is lost and we begin to use names and categories, we start putting value ratings upon each of the separate parts by calling them 'good' or 'bad'. Once we begin to think in terms of good and bad, it is very difficult to recapture the Oneness that is the reality of the universe.

There are already enough names.

We have dissected the world enough. We have separated people from each other so much by our classifications and categories that we have reached a point where we no longer see the humanity in others. As a result, exploitation and genocide have become common occurrences in our world.

Tao in the world is like a river flowing home to the sea.

The river is a symbol of Tai Chi. The river flows unceasingly towards its destiny, following its nature, making no effort, seeking nothing, always yielding, twisting, and turning to overcome the obstacles in its path. It brings benefit to the lives it touches.

By following its nature, it nourishes all that it comes into contact with. Thus, it is the perfect example for the Tai Chi person to emulate.

Verse 33

Knowing others is wisdom;
Knowing the self is enlightenment.

Understanding how other people think and feel is a developed state of awareness which very few people have the sensitivity to obtain. It is important for the Tai Chi person to understand what motivates other people's actions. Such understanding will help him to avoid conflict with others and will help him to see how he can aid others in their development.

However, understanding of oneself is an even higher level of knowledge. You are the Tao. Everything that is true for the Tao is true for you. If you can look within yourself, see the principles upon which your life moves, examine your fears, locate your strengths and weaknesses, then you will be able to understand how the universe works. The ego finds it hard to take such an experience. But this experience is required if we are ever to have the self-knowledge that will allow us to work upon those aspects of ourselves that keep us from the fullest development of our nature.

Tai Chi training gives the Tai Chi student both types of knowledge. By requiring that the student learns Tai Chi in a group, Tai Chi ensures that the student becomes sensitive to the moods and unique characteristics of the others. Each student has continuously to adapt and adjust his movements to the others. It is hoped that the student will have the same sensitivity to the people he passes on the street, sees at work, and those who wait for him at home.

Knowledge and understanding of others cannot be fully developed until the student has developed knowledge of the self, and every aspect of Tai Chi is designed to aid the student in this process. During the first lesson in Tai Chi, the student is taught to sink the rational mind into the Tan Tien, or Chi centre. There, the rational aspect of the mind is stilled as the mind merges with the body and serves as a receiver of unconscious impressions from the various parts of the body. In this state, the Tai Chi person becomes aware of all that is happening within himself. The result of this process is an intimate knowledge of himself and the ability to tap the inexhaustible source of Chi energy that lies at his centre.

Mastering others requires force;
Mastering the self needs strength.

Force and violence are required in order to control other people which shows how contrary to the Tao the desire to control others is. To master yourself, however, you need the inner strength that results from the uniting of the will with your Chi energy.

He who knows he has enough is rich.

Some people would consider themselves rich if they had a hundred thousand dollars while others would need a million, and some would never reach the point where they feel rich no matter how much money they had. Thus, the feeling of 'rich' has very little to do with the amount of money we possess. Richness is a mental state. We are rich when we reach a point where we realise that we have enough. Some people, because of greed, need for status, and fear of the future, will never reach that point. For other people, it comes even with very few material possessions.

Lao Tzu is saying that you should look closely at your life and realise that you have everything you need. Food and a warm place to sleep are the only material things you must have. Everything else you need to fulfil your destiny in life lies within you. Peace, tranquillity, harmony, and love are there for the taking in unlimited quantities. That is why very poor people can be rich and very rich people can be poor. In 1929, people threw themselves out of windows to their deaths because they lost their money in the stockmarket crash. They had a total lack of understanding of the meaning of wealth. Their lives were defined by their material possessions. When those possessions were lost, life became meaningless. By taking their lives, they gave up the treasures of a beautiful sunset, the golden laughter of a child, the smell of a forest after rain, and the human warmth of a family gathering. And all because they lost their swimming pools and their sports cars.

Perseverance is a sign of will power.

It demands a great deal of patience to learn Tai Chi. Tai Chi is a journey with no goals and no end. There are no awards or levels of achievement to mark the student's passage. The need for patience disappears only when the student has so integrated his life with the principles of Tai Chi that Tai Chi becomes something he is and not something he does.

He who stays where he is endures.

He who can hold to his centre passes through troubles untouched and unharmed.

Verse 35

All men will come to him who keeps to the one,
For there lie rest and happiness and peace.

The Tai Chi person is a refuge for those whom life has wounded. He is the rock that stands above the turbulent waters to which others can cling in times of trouble and pain. Because of his Oneness with the universe, he is an inexhaustible source of peace, rest, and happiness. To him all men are brothers to be cherished, nourished, and comforted without judgement of their worth. Without this all-encompassing compassion, the Tai Chi journey is impossible.

I have a student who is about 60 years old and overweight. He has been in my school for about six years. His movements are barely recognisable as Tai Chi movements and I know that he will never be able to do nice moves. But he is loved by the other students and to be around him is to feel the deep warmth and happiness emanating from within him. His joy of life and his ability to form a bond of friendship with everyone he meets makes him an ideal Tai Chi person. Thus, despite his movements, he is one of the pillars of my school. His love, joy, and compassion will take him to the Oneness that is his destiny.

I have another student who does some of the most beautiful moves that I have ever seen but who insists that she does not need other people and that other people do not need her. Though her Tai Chi movements are beautiful, as long as she cannot find the love and compassion that lie within her, she will never be able to enter the Tai Chi way of life. Without love and compassion, Tai Chi becomes mere gymnastics.

Verse 36

That which shrinks
Must first expand.
That which fails
Must first be strong.
That which is cast down
Must first be raised.

Opposites cannot be separated. There cannot be high without low, good without evil, rich without poor. Tai Chi teaches the student to avoid extremes in life; not to go too far and get the opposite of what he seeks. By not raising himself up on his toes, the student cannot be cast down. By not being strong and forceful, he cannot become tired and spent. By not being held high in the opinions of others, he need not worry about being cast down. The Tai Chi person seeks the middle point between opposites. In this middle point, neither of the opposites dominates the other. It is a place without high or low, good or bad, success or failure. In other words, it is a place of harmony.

Soft and weak overcome hard and strong.

In Tai Chi self-defence, the student relies on the softness and weakness of his body to overcome the aggression and strength of the attacker. In everyday life, the student relies on the softness and gentleness of his loving heart to overcome the hardness and strength of hatred and hostility.

Fish cannot leave deep waters...

Each individual must discover his own true nature and, once that nature is found, flow through life obeying its principles. A fish cannot leave water because living in water is its nature. If it lived on land, it would cease to be a fish. The Tai Chi person cannot leave compassion and love because compassion and love make up the nature of a human being. If a person can leave the qualities of love and compassion out of his life, he has ceased to be a human being. It is easy to recognise people who live the nature of the tiger, or of the fox, or of the snake.

And a country's weapons should not be displayed.

The display of weapons or of martial skill can cause fear and aggression in those around you. There will be those who feel helpless when confronted by your skill. In the back of their minds will always be the thought that you might hurt them. This thought could possibly keep them from trusting you.

Others will be challenged by your skill and will wish to see if they can overcome you. Neither of these reactions is desired by the Tai Chi person. Thus, it is very rare to see a Tai Chi self-defence demonstration. Recently, some teachers of Tai Chi have held tournaments and contests in order to demonstrate the skill of their students, and thus to advertise themselves as teachers. Such teachers have lost the very essence of what Tai Chi is. The Tai Chi person should go to great lengths to hide his skill.

Most of us in Tai Chi have become so adept at hiding our skill that some books about the martial arts say that Tai Chi cannot really be used for self-defence. There are two reasons for hiding this aspect of Tai Chi. The first is that we are not proud of our skill. Self-defence is the last resort for the Tai Chi person who has lost his Oneness with the Tao. It is a sign of failure, and victory is cause for shame.

The second reason is that if you have lost your harmony and conflict cannot be avoided, it is good if the attacker underestimates you. If the attacker thinks you are incapable of defending yourself, he will make mistakes he would not make if he believed you were very capable. And it is the attacker's mistakes that the Tai Chi person waits for. My school is next door to a judo and karate school. Occasionally when the karate students are leaving the building they look in at our door, see us doing Tai Chi, and leave with a smirk on their faces at our obvious lack of strength and fighting skill. This is exactly what we wish others to think.

Verse 37

Tao abides in non-action,
Yet nothing is left undone.

Tai Chi is based in the concept of Wu Wei, of simply letting things take their natural course, of letting yourself act spontaneously. When the mind does not interfere with the body, the Tai Chi person flows through the movements without effort. When human beings do not interfere with the universe, all things flow in harmony with the principles of the Tao without effort.

If kings and lords observed this,
The ten thousand things would develop naturally.

If governments understood the way of Wu Wei, there would be much less conflict and much more freedom in the world.

If they still desired to act,
They would return to the simplicity of formless substance.
Without form there is no desire.

If we do not follow the principle of Wu Wei (that is, allowing our actions to be determined by our desires and ambitions), our lives remain trapped within the boundaries set by the ideas and definitions to which our egos have become attached. To escape this trap, the Tai Chi person returns to the simplicity of formlessness. In other words, he must abandon the set ideas, ambitions, and desires that have 'formed' him into someone definable. When these are gone, he becomes 'formless', which means that his actions arise spontaneously in a natural reaction to everything he encounters. Because our desires arise from our fixed view of the world and from our ambitions, the absence of such a view and of ambitions frees us from desires.

Verse 40

Returning is the motion of the Tao.

The Tao is a circle. In its moving, every point in the Tao returns to its original position over and over. This implies that when an opportunity is missed, there is no need to go chasing after it, but rather the person should wait alert, aware, and ready to move in any direction at any second until the opportunity returns. This is true for all aspects of life. If you wish to marry and miss your opportunity, you do not rush through life trying to force all the women you meet to be the right woman. You must wait until the right woman appears and be sensitive enough to recognise her when she does. Trying to force the universe into situations that you desire only leads to catastrophe.

Westerners are not accustomed to this way of understanding the world. Thus, Western businessmen often have problems when dealing with Orientals. A Western businessman makes a decision and then wants immediate action. When he makes a deal with an oriental firm and nothing seems to be happening, he attributes this to laziness, or lack of competence. But the oriental businessman is simply waiting for circumstances to arise that would insure the success of his endeavours.

This principle of 'waiting for the Tao' is the basic element of Tai Chi self-defence. The karate person tries to force an opening to his opponent with his strength and skill, but the Tai Chi person waits for an opportunity to present itself. When an opportunity does arise, such as when the aggressor has become over-extended, the Tai Chi person strikes instantly. If his strike misses, he does not try to keep striking, but withdraws and awaits the next opportunity.

Yielding is the way of the Tao.

Water yields to the rock in its path, yet eventually wears the rock down. This is the way of Tai Chi, both in self-defence and in everyday life. When aggression or hardness, whether spiritual, mental, or physical, is met, the Tai Chi person yields until their force is spent.

The ten thousand things are born of being.

All that exists (the ten thousand things) was created by the uniting of Yin and Yang Chi. Thus, the Chi is the vital energy that flows in all things. When I can connect my Chi with the Chi of an object, or of another person, I can become one with that object or person, because, though we are different manifestations of the Tao, the Chi within us is the same.

Being is born of not being.

The Chi, the Yin and Yang, arise from the Nothingness, the Void which is the Tao. We exist as individual entities by virtue of our unique combination of Chi energy, but at our centre is the Void. It is in the Void that all things touch and become one. For centuries, the Asians have considered the ability to enter the Void and remain there to be the highest level of spiritual development. This is the

Nirvana of the Buddhists. It is also the highest level of self-defence in the martial arts. Reaching the Void means that the student cannot be harmed. What can harm emptiness? In the Void, the Tai Chi person becomes completely one with the attacker. As soon as the attacker makes a Yang movement, the Tai Chi person automatically makes a Yin movement. The attacker cannot make a move without a complementary move being made by the Tai Chi person. The Tai Chi person can only be harmed if the attacker can bring him out of the Void by causing him to become angry or afraid. Anger and fear sink us into the ego and make us lose our Oneness with the Void. The ego is the barrier that keeps us out of the Void and separated from others.

Verse 42

The Tao begot one.

From the Tao came existence.

One begot two.

Existence was manifested in the Yin and Yang Chi.

Two begot three.

From the combination of Yin and Yang Chi came heaven, earth, and humanity.

And three begot the ten thousand things.

All that exists is the creation of heaven, earth, or human beings.

The ten thousand things carry yin and embrace yang.
They achieve harmony by combining these forces.

Everything that exists has Yin and Yang Chi and achieves a harmonious state within itself by balancing them. Tai Chi is designed to achieve such balance. The longer a person practises Tai Chi, the more internal changes occur as the Yin and Yang Chi reach an ever more balanced state. Those people who are too Yin, who have a weakness of will and spirit, develop a confidence and self-assuredness as the Yang increases. Those people who are too Yang, who are aggressive and insensitive, develop the Yin qualities of compassion and open-heartedness.

Men hate to be 'orphaned', 'widowed', or 'worthless',
But this is how kings and lords describe themselves.

In order to have the support and trust of the country, those who exercise power in the government must identify themselves with the humblest of the population. To be seen riding in limousines and living in palatial houses only causes resentment, envy, and distrust in those whom the politician seeks to lead. If it is someone's nature to be a servant of the people, he needs no reward for serving. If it is not his nature, then he should not be in office. How could you trust such a person to put the welfare of the people above his own ambitions? If politicians were required to live in the same circumstances as those of the poorest citizen, the plight of the poorest in our societies would be improved very quickly.

The above is also true for the employer. If he would identify with the lowest of his employees, feel his needs and desires, the employee would be much more willing to give his best.

> *For one gains by losing*
> *And loses by gaining.*

By losing your attachment to things, you gain freedom. By gaining possessions, fame, or wealth, you become tied to them and freedom is lost.

What others teach, I also teach; that is:
'A violent man will die a violent death!'
This will be the essence of my teaching.

These words are the heart of the Tai Chi message. Violence is a separation from the person to whom you are committing the violence, from your own human nature, and from the principles of the Tao. You cannot violate the principles of the Tao without meeting a disastrous fate. Thus, in Tai Chi, we try to avoid harming others at almost any cost even when defending ourselves from physical attack.

Verse 43

The softest thing in the universe
Overcomes the hardest thing in the universe.

A deeply felt love that expresses itself in compassion, profound sympathy, mercy, and empathy is the softest thing in the universe, but with it the Tai Chi person can overcome hate, which is the hardest thing in the universe. This love is the Tai Chi person's shield and treasure. It will protect him from the hostility of others and it will be his guide on his journey to his destiny. Love is the first and highest level of self-defence in Tai Chi. When the Tai Chi person can apply it successfully, he will need no other type of self-defence because, at that level, he will be able to walk into a hostile situation and strip away the hostility with his love.

That without substance can enter where there is no room.

The person who has given up ambition, the ego, and prejudices can fit into any situation, including another's closed heart.

Hence I know the value of non-action.

The Tai Chi person must learn the value of spontaneous movement, of doing only that which flows from his nature.

Teaching without words and work without doing
Are understood by very few.

Of all the people who begin the discipline of Tai Chi, only a handful will continue past a year or so. Humility, compassion, lack of ambition, non-aggression, spontaneity, and silence are not qualities that our societies value. There is no more difficult journey than the journey to the self.

Verse 44

Fame or self: which matters more?

Fame is a type of definition applied to the person who possesses it. People expect certain types of behaviour from the famous and therefore the famous always feel the pressure to behave in such a way as to reinforce their fame. As a result, it is very difficult for the famous person to be himself because he is always trying to live the role that his fame has defined for him. Fame also causes envy and resentment in others. Hence, the Tai Chi person avoids fame as 'unnecessary baggage' on his journey to himself.

Self or wealth: which is more precious?

Which is worth more to you: to have lots of money and possessions, or to discover the secrets of your own nature and the destiny toward which it leads you? The journey your nature takes you on may lead you through poverty, but it is a journey that must be made if you are to reach the harmony, tranquillity, and peace that is your destiny.

Gain or loss: which is more painful?

The Tai Chi person must have total freedom in order to follow his nature wherever it leads him. Possessions take away freedom. People become possessed by their possessions. Possessions can be disastrous for the leading of a Tai Chi life. But the loss of the ego, of prejudices, and of fixed ideas gives freedom and eases the journey of Tai Chi.

He who is attached to things will suffer much.

The universe is continually changing. Nothing ever remains the same. Everyone and everything must eventually return to the Void. Therefore, the Tai Chi person must remain unattached. This has especial reference concerning people we love. Most people love others because of what those others can do for them. We are possessive of our loved ones and we seek to bind them to us. The Tai Chi person must give his love while remaining unattached. He must love others not because of what they do for him but because they are themselves. Unlike jealous love, which seeks to bind, the love of the Tai Chi person is a liberating love. The love of the true Tai Chi person remains regardless of what changes occur in the behaviour or character of the beloved. The beloved knows that no matter what changes he or she goes through, the love of the Tai Chi person will always be there.

Possessive love is not true love. If the beloved is meant to be with you, you need no cage to keep them. If they leave you, they were never yours anyway. I use this approach with my Tai Chi students: if they do not have to be in my school, then they should leave and look for their true teacher.

He who saves will suffer heavy loss.

The journey to the Tao is anything but secure. Security is the death of freedom. People spend so much of their time trying to make their lives secure that they have no time to live. The Tai Chi journey is a journey without guides and without maps. It is an entirely different journey for everyone who makes it. No one knows the way to the Tao. Every second of his life, the Tai Chi person stands at a crossroads with many different roads lying before him. Every step of the journey is a gamble and the Tai Chi person must be willing to risk everything (that is, the love of friends and family, health, possessions, status in society) in order to follow his nature to where it leads him.

A contented man is never disappointed.

When a person's contentment arises from within himself and not from external factors, it cannot be taken away from him. Such a person is concerned only with the unfolding of his life in a process that leads him ever deeper into knowledge of himself and of the Tao. This process is what makes up his life and all other factors, such as financial position, social status, fame, etc., have no meaning for him and are without importance because, no matter how these external factors may change, the journey goes on and it is in the journey that he has his being.

He who knows when to stop does not find himself in trouble.
He will stay forever safe.

Going to extremes causes loss of balance and rootedness. The Tai Chi person must always have balance in order to respond to life with 100 per cent of his power.

Verse 45

Great accomplishment seems imperfect...

To the Tai Chi person, the greatest accomplishment possible is to become one with his own nature and to flow with that nature to his destiny. If that means he should become a woodcutter rather than a famous scientist or a movie star, then he will be a woodcutter. But to the society he finds himself in, being a woodcutter is not held in high regard, and thus this accomplishment seems imperfect. People cannot understand why he would be a woodcutter when he could be a movie star. That is because our society respects social status rather than personal contentment and happiness.

Yet it does not outlive its usefulness.

Though money and fame may be lost, achieving Oneness with the self and the harmony and tranquillity that are a result of Oneness lasts forever.

Great fullness seems empty.

When people are filled with the ego, prejudices, and ambition, they have ordinary fullness. 'Great fullness' is the fullness of love, compassion, non-violence, and self-knowledge. Our societies have no respect for such fullness. There are always job advertisements in the paper for aggressive, ambitious young men and women. But when did you ever see a job advertisement for a person with deep self-knowledge and compassion?

Great intelligence seems stupid.

The knowledge that our Western societies value is the knowledge of facts. Modern life is a constant accumulation of facts and information. The more technological we become, the faster the human being must move in order to stay on top of the process. The more facts a person can retain and manipulate, the more he is rewarded and respected. The problem of this mere knowledge of facts is that facts are meaningless without a deep understanding of life. For example, I can know the exact number of metric tons of wheat in surplus storage in the United States and the exact number of people starving in Ethiopia. But, these facts are meaningless unless a deep well of compassion is within me that will lead me to the obvious path of action that these facts point to.

Such knowledge of life is the 'great intelligence' that Lao Tzu is speaking of. The poor farmer in South America who knows how to avoid the extremes of ideology, who knows how to adjust to the environment, and who lives his life out in humility, has this knowledge of life. And yet, our society would consider him stupid because he does not know how a computer works, or the name of the president of the United States. On the other hand, we honour and reward the scientist who has discovered a new fact even though he is an alcoholic, beats his wife, and has a son addicted to drugs. We do not care that he has no understanding of life. The world continues to make giant strides in technology and the speed with which information can be transferred, but fails to achieve the harmony, peace, and tranquillity that would make these advances truly beneficial.

Knowledge of life and how it works is the foundation upon which Tai Chi is based. As the student learns to know himself and becomes ever more sensitive to what is happening within, the principles that guide all life are revealed and the intuitive knowledge that lies within us all is allowed to surface. It is only when this intuitive understanding is fully developed that the student can really practise Tai Chi. Tai Chi cannot be done with the rational mind and thus, cannot be taught. The teacher can only guide the student through the moves until the student reaches the point where he intuitively understands what Tai Chi is.

Great eloquence seems awkward.

Zen poetry seems awkward to the Westerner because the poet uses few words. The meaning of the Zen poem is conveyed by what is not said, and yet it conveys the essence of life more clearly than other types of poetry. Tai Chi also has this awkwardness as the teacher tries to teach that which cannot be taught and to speak about that which cannot be spoken. The student must learn to hear the silence surrounding the teacher's loss of words. In the silence, the Tao speaks for itself.

Movement overcomes cold.
Stillness overcomes heat.

Movement overcomes stagnation. Stillness overcomes the violent swinging back and forth between desires. The Tai Chi person must continually move (that is, develop and grow), while at the same time always remain still (that is, fixed to his immovable centre). Thus, Tai Chi is often called 'The Unmoving Movement',

Stillness and tranquillity set things in order in the universe.

It is only in stillness and tranquillity that we can feel and see the Oneness and harmony of the universe.

Verse 46

When the Tao is present in the universe,
The horses haul manure.
When the Tao is absent from the universe,
War horses are bred outside the city.

When Oneness with the Tao has been achieved, there is peace, tranquillity, and harmony and everything fulfils its nature in such a way that there is no violence or conflict. But when the harmony of the Tao is lost, the nature of everything becomes perverted. In such a situation, the horse, with its ability to aid the farmer and to make human life easier, becomes an instrument of war and death. Human nature also becomes perverted when the Tao is lost. The love, compassion, and mercy that is the heart of human nature becomes lost in racism, religious hatred, alienation from others, and competition in all aspects of life.

There is no greater sin than desire...

By sin, Lao Tzu means error. The error of desire leads you away from your centre and causes you to violate your natural path in order to obtain the object of your desire.

No greater curse than discontent...

Being unhappy with your state in life prevents you from reaching tranquillity and harmony. There are people who spend their entire lives going from one goal to the next hoping that each successive achievement will somehow end the discontent that is at the centre of their existence. But contentment is not something that lies outside the person. It is not something that can be achieved. Contentment is something that must be realised through knowledge of the self and a life surrounded by love and compassion for others.

No greater misfortune than wanting something for oneself.

This misfortune is total separation from others and is called 'selfishness'. It is the curse of human history. Our history of violence, greed, and environmental destruction will not change until selfishness has been abandoned. There are many active, motivated people who struggle against oppression, or who fight for a more just economic system, or who seek to protect the environment, or who lead crusades against drug addiction, etc. But all these problems are merely symptoms of the disease of selfishness. Fighting the problems of the world by attacking each individual one is like cutting the limbs of the tree in order to get rid of the tree. A new limb will grow again in some other place. The root must be dug up if you wish to get rid of the tree. Perhaps you can win equal rights for women. Perhaps you can stop the polluting of rivers. Perhaps you can end racial discrimination. However, these problems will only be replaced by others because the disease is still there.

To accept the Tai Chi way of life is to accept full responsibility for the world. It is up to the Tai Chi person to re-establish the harmony of the Tao in the world by ridding himself of selfishness. In so doing, he or she becomes the teacher, the silent example for others. He leaves the great conquests and crusades for others and contents himself with the daily, silent, agonising struggle with his own selfishness, knowing that this is the only way he can truly help the world. Selfish people do not last very long in Tai Chi. They either change or they leave. I have had such people in my school. They become very clannish with the other students in their class and resentful when new members or visitors come to the class, or they strive with the other students to see who performs the best movements. The spirit of Tai Chi usually overcomes their selfishness very quickly, otherwise they must be eased gently and quietly out of the school.

Therefore he who knows that enough is enough
will always have enough.

When you lose your desires and attachments to things outside yourself, then what you have will be enough.

Verse 47

Without going outside, you may know the whole world.
Without looking through the window,
you may see the ways of heaven.
The farther you go, the less you know.

The Tao is the macrocosm and the individual human being is the microcosm. Everything that occurs in the universe occurs within ourselves. By looking within ourselves, we can discover the principles that guide the universe and that are the foundation of Tai Chi. Through the discipline of Tai Chi, the Tai Chi person draws ever closer to self-understanding and self-awareness. As the student learns to become one with his body and begins to understand how it can be united with. his will he starts to discover his own unique nature and the principles that guide it and, in so doing, he reaches the heart of Tai Chi. Thus, Tai Chi is a journey within ourselves toward the centre; toward the source. The further away we are from that source, the more we are attracted to external things, the less understanding it will be possible for us to have.

Thus the sage knows without travelling...

Pilgrimages, gurus, holy books, rituals, and even Tai Chi are not necessary for the journey to Oneness and harmony. These things, including Tai Chi, are merely mirrors which reflect your inner self. You can do without any of them (including this volume) simply by turning within yourself and tapping your intuitive knowledge.

He sees without looking...

The Tai Chi student searches for and finds the way within himself. He learns to see not just with the eyes, but with his total being. His entire body, soul, and mind become sensitised so that he 'sees without looking'. This sensitising process is a vital part of Tai Chi and begins with the first lessons. The first two months or so are spent in practising flexibility exercises, balancing exercises, and breathing exercises. These exercises help the student to get in touch with the various parts of his body. As a result, these parts of the body can communicate with him. He learns to listen to his body, knowing that it will tell him when his movements are wrong. His legs will tell him when he is off balance. His lungs will tell him if he should breathe in or out with a particular movement and at what speed he should breathe in order to make the breath one with the movement.

In the beginning, students have difficulty maintaining the same tempo during the moves. Beginners look around a lot to see where everyone is. This is especially the case when the student is the last person on the left or the right. When the group turns left or right, there is no one for this student to look at. How can the student keep the speed of the group when he cannot see the others? The only way he can do it is by being sensitive enough to feel the energy flow of the group.

Such sensitivity is of great benefit in both self-defence and everyday life. In self-defence the action is so fast that you cannot see all that is happening. You must feel what the opponent is going to do before he does it.

Since there are no maps, books, or gurus that can lead the student to the Tao, every step he takes is a vital decision. The Tai Chi person must be sensitive to all aspects of the situation around him in order to feel his way through. As the student becomes more and more sensitive, he will see this process operating in his life and will learn to trust it.

Between 1978 and 1980, I spent ten months on a kibbutz in Israel studying Hebrew. Late one night, I was sitting in my room studying, when I felt something pulling my attention away from my book. I got up, went to the door, and looked out. There was a young woman standing about 20 yards away. I went to her and I could see that she had been crying. We began to talk and she told me about her problems with her boyfriend. I went back into my room and brought out a bar of chocolate that I keep for such emergencies and we went for a walk. We had an excellent time joking and laughing and by the time I left her, she was in a very happy mood.

Another time on the kibbutz, I was walking past the living quarters when I felt something that caused me to look at one of the houses. A young woman was sitting on the porch of the house crying silently. I went to her and listened to her problems. I took her to my room where some friends of mine were playing cards and I asked them to let her into the game. I left to milk the cows, which was my work on the kibbutz. When I came home she was sitting with the others laughing and enjoying the evening. To heal pain, to overcome loneliness, to ease the path of others is the role of the Tai Chi person, because their pain and loneliness is his. But before he can do these things, he must have sensitised his whole being to the point where he can 'see without looking'.

He works without doing.

The Tai Chi person does only that which his nature demands that he does and therefore his actions are without goal or ambition. His actions are not something he does, but rather, something that flows from within him.

Verse 48

In the pursuit of learning, every day something is acquired.

Our society praises and rewards the type of learning that results in the acquiring of new facts. The more facts you command, the more useful you are to society. Thus, to remain competitive and successful, you must continuously acquire new information. This process continues until you can no longer keep up and then society shoves you aside as useless to let you live out your life with the fading memories of your successes.

In the pursuit of Tao, every day something is dropped.

The Tai Chi person is engaged in a different type of learning in which things are lost rather than acquired. During his journey, he will lose his ego, his preconceived ideas about the world, his prejudices, his selfishness, his ambition, and his aggression. Such a journey is neither respected nor rewarded by society, but brings the fulfilment of his nature.

Less and less is done
Until non-action is achieved.

The longer the Tai Chi student practises his discipline, the more the philosophy and psychology of Tai Chi permeates his being. He begins to see life differently and his ambitions and goals begin to fall away. With time, everything he does will flow spontaneously from his nature. When that happens, 'non-action is achieved'.

When nothing is done, nothing is left undone.

Everything in nature acts spontaneously. Spontaneity is the way of the Tao and it is the way of Tai Chi. When all things flow naturally and spontaneously, then no further action is required. Everything we need is provided for by the Tao without effort on our part. In Tai Chi, the less you think about what you are doing, the less you make a conscious effort, the closer you come to true Tai Chi.

The world is ruled by letting things take their course.
It cannot be ruled by interfering.

The Tao rules all things by allowing everything to follow its own nature. It does not interfere with the principles that guide all things. Only human beings interfere and therefore it is we who are responsible for the harmony of the universe because only we can destroy it.

Tai Chi is also an order that allows the student to move according to his own nature. As such, it must not be interfered with. Teachers who try to adapt it for a purpose such as dancing, or merely for health reasons, only destroy it.

Verse 49

The sage has no mind of his own.
He is aware of the needs of others.

The Tai Chi person must have no opinions that he espouses and tries to force upon others. He can only teach by example, and thus his life is his teaching. His mind must be as open as his heart and as flexible as his body. Hence, the true Tai Chi person has no fear of strange ideas nor of the people who possess these ideas.

Nevertheless, the Tai Chi person realises that others are not like him. Others have a need to think the way they do because their ideas and beliefs offer them security. If he were to threaten their ideas, anger and conflict would result. The Tai Chi person keeps his opinions to himself and tries to guide by example alone. This is especially true for the Tai Chi teacher who must teach people from various backgrounds. It is a very difficult self-discipline that is required to remain silent while others are espousing ideas that you consider to be completely inaccurate and even harmful, but it is a self-discipline that the Tai Chi person must possess in order to establish harmony with all whom he meets.

I am good to people who are good.
I am also good to people who are not good.

By being good to others, Lao Tzu means that you react to all people from your nature. Human nature is love and compassion. The Tai Chi person reacts to all people with love and compassion whether those people are showing love and compassion towards him or not. Since he is one with his nature, he has no other choice. If he can react in any other manner, then he has not achieved oneness with his nature. The Tai Chi person is like the river that quenches the thirst of the saint and the murderer equally because that is its nature.

I have faith in people who are faithful.
I also have faith in people who are not faithful.

The same idea applies to faith as applies to goodness. The Tai Chi person has faith in the Tao and the progress of human development, and that all people will reach a state of harmony with the universe. This faith is not something that can be turned off or on but arises from human nature.

The sage is shy and humble – to the world he seems confusing.

The Tai Chi person does not push himself forward in an effort to gain admiration or fame. In order to avoid conflict and offence to others, he seeks the lowest places. The values of our society are exactly the opposite. The Tai Chi person therefore may seem confusing to the society around him.

Men look to him and listen.

He rarely speaks and when he does speak he has something to say. His humility, tranquillity, and peace are greatly needed by the world and because of them all people are attracted to him.

He behaves like a little child.

The Tai Chi person reacts to the world spontaneously just as small children do and, like the child, the world is ever new and interesting because nothing is categorised and pre-judged.

Verse 50

Between birth and death,
Three in ten are followers of life...

These people are moving toward realisation of their nature and Oneness with the Tao.

Three in ten are followers of death...

These people thrive on separation, competition and conflict. They cannot become one with the flow of life.

And men just passing from birth to death also number three in ten.

These people spend their lives wavering between the way of life and the way of death.

Why is this so?
Because they live their lives on the gross level.

Many people live lives completely controlled by their desires and attachments. These people are unable to see the Oneness and awesomeness of the universe. For them, there is no room for vision, imagination, or anything except self-gratification.

He who knows how to live can walk abroad
Without fear of rhinoceros or tiger.
He will not be wounded in battle.
For in him rhinoceroses can find no place to thrust their horn,
Tigers no place to use their claws,
And weapons no place to pierce.
Why is this so?
Because he has no place for death to enter.

The harmony of the Tao depends upon everything in the universe establishing a harmonious relationship with everything else. The harmony of the whole depends upon the harmony of each part. Therefore, the harmony of the universe depends upon you as an individual manifestation of the Tao. Without you fulfilling your role in the Tao, the totality is lost. In such a state, you are unimportant to the universe and when you die is of no consequence. After all, you are not going anywhere anyway. If you are not moving toward your destiny, then your life is meaningless and your death might as well be also. But once you have committed yourself to finding your nature, you are moving toward your destiny, that unique place in the universe, that unique function that you, alone, are to perform. In such circumstances, the universe is with you and everything that exists will aid you on your journey because the harmony of all depends upon your success. You need not fear death until your destiny has been fulfilled. Until then, nothing will harm you and death has no place to enter. And when death does come it will be full of meaning, as the final statement of all that you have been.

The perfect example of such a meaningful death is that of Mahatma Gandhi. He died at the perfect time, after having shown the world the way of non-violence: his death was the final summation of his teaching.

I feel that I know my destiny and, thus, I have no fear of death because I know I cannot die until I have done what my nature demands that I do.

Verse 51

All things arise from Tao.
They are nourished by Virtue.

Everything is nourished by the essence of its nature which is the Tao, the Yin and Yang Chi.

They are formed from matter.
They are shaped by environment.
Thus the ten thousand things all respect Tao and honour Virtue.

Respect of Tao and honour of Virtue are not demanded,
But they are in the nature of things.

We are formed by the combination of Yin and Yang Chi, but our lives are shaped by the society in which we are reared. As we grow older, we take on the ideas, prejudices, and fears of the community we live in. But at our core is the Void that unites us with all other things to form the Tao. It is in the nature of all things to yearn for the harmony and peace that comes with Oneness.

Therefore all things arise from Tao.
By Virtue they are nourished,
Developed, cared for,
Sheltered, comforted,
Grown, protected.
Creating without claiming,
Doing without taking credit,
Guiding without interfering,
This is Primal Virtue.

These lines are a description of the Tao and of the Tai Chi person. The Tai Chi person helps everything and everyone to grow and develop toward their own nature. He is the father of the earth and the female Tai Chi person is the mother of all things. In him and her all things find shelter, comfort, and protection. They create without claiming because they are unattached and because what they do comes from their nature and not from the ego. They guide all things by their example. When they are capable of these things, they have reached the highest state of humanity – the Primal Virtue being the First Principle.

Verse 52

The beginning of the universe
Is the mother of all things.

The Tao is the Great Female, the Great Mother. The Tao provides all that you need and guides you through life as long as you obey its principles. And, like a mother, it loves all its children equally. The Tai Chi teacher, imitating the Tao, must have a compassionate love for all of his students.

Knowing the mother, one also knows the sons.

If you understand how the universe moves and develops, you will also understand how individual objects and persons move and develop because the same principles that guide the whole guide the individual parts. And these are the principles that Tai Chi tries to help the student to discover.

Knowing the sons, yet remaining in touch with the mother,
Brings freedom from the fear of death.

Knowing and working with the individual objects and people of which the universe is made up, the Tai Chi person does not lose sight of the Oneness that unites them all with himself. Though the individual object or person may die, the Tao goes on forever, and as a part of this Oneness, the individual can never be lost.

The following lines of this verse are advice to the Tai Chi person for his dealing with the 'sons':

Keep your mouth shut...

Words cannot transmit truth. Only experience can do that. The Tai Chi person should pass through life as silently as possible. His life speaks for itself.

Guard the senses...

Avoid attachment to objects and people. A life spent trying to fulfil one desire after the other only makes for a busy life that draws the person ever further away from his centre. Such a life is beyond hope of tranquillity and peace.

Seeing the small is insight...

A journey of 1,000 miles begins with one step. Do not look ahead, but focus on each small step and in time the journey will be finished. In other words, pay attention to the small things in life and the big things will take care of themselves. In Tai Chi, it is not the large movements that are difficult to master, but the small, subtle ones. The Tai Chi student must breathe correctly, feel the balance with his entire body, relax all the various parts of his body, and the movements will flow naturally and spontaneously without effort.

Yielding to force is strength.

Yielding to avoid force and aggression in the belief that the weakness of love and compassion overcomes the strength of anger and violence is the strength of the Tai Chi person.

Using the outer light, return to insight,
And in this way be saved from harm.

By observing the world around him and noting the principles that guide all things, the Tai Chi person gains insight into his nature. Tai Chi seeks to make the student perceptive and sensitive enough to make this process possible.

Verse 54

What is firmly established cannot be uprooted.
What is firmly grasped cannot slip away.

When the Tai Chi student has found his centre and holds to it, when his life has become rooted in and permeated by love and compassion, he cannot be moved by the violence and aggression of the world around him. He stands like a mountain facing all that life brings to him. This ability is what makes him the refuge of others in times of trouble. It is this immovable position that makes him free from fear and allows him to love all things.

This idea of rootedness is very important in Tai Chi self-defence. Tai Chi instruction is very concerned with the footwork upon which the movements are based. If the stance is not correct, there can be no balance. The entire body rests upon the feet. If the feet are not in the correct position, then correct breathing, hand movement, focus, and co-ordination will mean nothing because the movement will have no base from which to flow. The weight must be correctly distributed between the two feet and the feet must be rooted to the ground. This rootedness is achieved by sending Chi from the Tan Tien (Chi centre) through the legs into the ground. The teacher should be able to push the student at any time during the Tai Chi sequence without the student losing his balance.

It is the same with life. We should be so rooted in our harmony and our nature that no push from the world around us can dislodge us from our non-violence, compassion, and peace. Everyone has met people who are friendly, helpful, and loving when everything is all right, but who lose these qualities in times of stress. That is because their lives are not rooted.

Verse 55

He who is filled with Virtue is like a newborn child.

To the child, the world is Oneness. The child sees no separation between himself and his mother or between himself and the toy he holds in his hand. Everything he touches becomes an extension of himself. This is the state towards which the Tai Chi student returns.

> *Wasps and serpents will not sting him;*
> *Wild beasts will not pounce upon him;*
> *He will not be attacked by birds of prey.*

Once you have become one with your nature and are flowing towards your destiny, the universe moves with you, aiding your every step; nothing will be allowed to harm you because the universe needs you to find your place in the great harmony and to perform that unique task which you alone can do. A student once asked me how we can know when we are going the correct way. When what you are doing comes easily and naturally to you, then you know this is your way. If what you are doing requires great effort and you seem to be continuously blocked, then chances are that you are going the wrong way. But the only real way to know is to look within yourself to see if what you are doing is something you have to do. If it is something that your nature demands that you do, then it does not matter if there is difficulty or not, or if it is right or wrong for you.

His bones are soft, his muscles weak,
But his grip is firm.

The infant has little muscular strength and yet his grip is strong. His strength comes from the uniting of his will with his Chi. In Tai Chi, we do no muscle exercises in order to strengthen ourselves. Tai Chi men are not the large, muscular, hard men of karate. Our strength, like the child's, depends upon our ability to will something and then to move towards it with 100 per cent of our body, mind, soul, and energy. We shall never be admired physical specimens, but it is not admiration that the Tai Chi person seeks.

He has not experienced the union of man and woman, but is whole.
His manhood is strong.

The child has not experienced the sexual union of man and woman but the male and female are united within him. He has not yet learned to differentiate between man and woman. He has not assumed the societal role and prejudices of his sex. He is complete in his Oneness. And though he has not experienced sexual union, he is capable of having an erection.

Using the child as an example, the Tai Chi man does not reject the female part of him and the Tai Chi woman does not reject her male aspect. All Yang has some Yin and all Yin has some Yang. Society teaches men to suppress their 'female' qualities, like deep emotion and intuitive feeling, child rearing, etc., and it teaches women to suppress their 'male' qualities, like self-confidence, independence, and physical courage. The Tai Chi person tries to balance the Yin and Yang energies that are his essence.

He screams all day without becoming hoarse.
This is perfect harmony.

A little child can scream all day without becoming hoarse but an adult becomes hoarse after a very short time. Why is this? It is because the child does whatever he does with his whole being and holds back nothing. Thus, his screaming is natural and spontaneous. The adult, on the other hand, screams like he does everything else; with only a part of himself and thus has no deep source of power to draw upon.

Knowing harmony is constancy.
Knowing constancy is enlightenment.

Once the Tai Chi person has managed to become centred within himself and achieved harmony and tranquillity in his life, he can remain unmoved no matter what is happening around him. This is constancy. The Tai Chi person's harmony comes from within himself and thus cannot be disturbed by what is occurring on the outside.

One of the biggest problems in self-defence is the fear and panic that occurs when you are attacked. Panic causes tension and slows responses. Thus, the Tai Chi person must train himself to the point where he is so rooted in his centre and in his tranquillity that an attack, no matter how ferocious, will not be able to move him from his equilibrium.

Only with this constancy can we see clearly. When we are knocked back and forth by events, we see only what our emotions and prejudices allow us to see. Seeing things as they are, unattached to the results of our actions, unmoved from our centre, is the highest state of enlightenment.

It is not wise to rush about.

Many people are in such a hurry to accomplish things in life that they miss life altogether. Such people have no time for understanding before they act. They have no time to search deep within themselves for the meaning of things. They have no time to get to know the hearts of others and to find the Oneness with them. They have no time to learn the rhythms of nature so that they might adapt themselves to it rather than forcing nature to adapt to them. Such busy people will never have the patience to make the Tai Chi journey.

Controlling the breath causes strain.

Tai Chi never goes to excess in anything. Over-extension, using the Chi energy without restraint, straining the muscles, etc., is competition with and separation from the self. Sometimes I see students who make a great deal of noise with their breathing. They are forcing the breath rather than allowing it to flow naturally. The breath should be as silent as the rest of Tai Chi.

If too much energy is used, exhaustion follows.
This is not the way of Tao.
Whatever is contrary to Tao will not last long.

All muscular strength has its limits. Everything done with effort expends energy. There is a point where the energy of effort must fail whether it is muscular energy, spiritual energy, or mental energy. The Tai Chi person does things naturally and spontaneously without effort and can tap the Chi energy at his centre, which is infinite. This is the way of Tao.

Verse 56

Those who know do not talk.
Those who talk do not know.

Truth is beyond ideas and words: it can only be experienced. People who spend their time talking about truth, enlightenment, and wisdom cannot possibly know what they are talking about, or they would not make the effort – and that includes me. (I do not presume that this book will help anyone. I write it only because I feel it is something I have to do.) This leads to great difficulty for Tai Chi teachers. In Tai Chi, there is no supreme authority. People who obtain the highest level of Tai Chi development will never be known because they know better than to teach that which cannot be taught. Thus, any teacher you meet is someone who has not yet reached the Tao. The Tai Chi teacher is a person who has been on the Tai Chi journey for a number of years and thus (you hope) knows a little. But the student must be aware that the teacher does not know the way, he does not know Tai Chi or he would not be teaching. Who can teach the Tao? Who can know the universe?

The student finds a teacher whom he thinks knows a little, and when he has learned all that he can from that teacher he finds someone who can take him further. And so forth. If the student endures on the journey, he finally reaches a point where he knows a little, and can teach it to others. But when he reaches the highest levels, when he becomes one with the Tao, there is no more teacher and there is no more student. There is only the Void into which the Tai Chi person vanishes.

Keep your mouth closed.

The Tao and Tai Chi are most readily experienced in silence.

Guard your senses.

Do not let your desires and attachments sway you from your journey.

Temper your sharpness.

Whatever it is about you that harms other people or that makes them feel ill at ease, get rid of it.

Simplify your problems.

Life is really very simple, as nature demonstrates, but human beings like to make things complex. We need something to make us feel important (that is, money, fame, power). If you are very poor and have no power, the only thing that can make you feel more important than others is race or religion. With all the divisions and classifications we use to try to make ourselves seem important, life becomes very complicated. The average life expectancy is about 75 years and in this extremely short span of time we do so much to make life bothersome and complicated for each other. Simply look within yourself and realise what the essentials of life are and abandon all the extras and life will be much better for everyone.

Mask your brightness.

If your intellect intimidates others, dampen it in order to avoid conflict. If your wealth causes envy, make no show of it. If your fame causes jealousy, do not brag of your achievements.

Be at one with the dust of the earth.

Humility is the basis of Tai Chi. The Tai Chi person exists only to serve others, to protect life, and to help the universe to obtain harmony.

He who has achieved this state
Is unconcerned with friends and enemies,
With good and harm, with honour and disgrace.
This therefore is the highest state of man.

When the Tai Chi person has obtained Oneness with himself and with the universe, he does only that which his nature demands that he do and he does not worry if his actions will please his friends or create enemies, whether they will bring him honour or disgrace. This is the highest level of development for human beings and at this point the Tai Chi person disappears into the Void.

Verse 59

In caring for others and serving heaven,
There is nothing like using restraint.

The Tai Chi person helps the universe to reach a state of harmony and peace. To do this he must care for others, but not to excess. To go too far is to find the opposite of that which you seek. To care for someone excessively is to take away their responsibility for themselves. Restraint begins by giving up one's own ideas about how things should be, and accepting things as they are. Only when we see things as they truly are can we help others.

This depends on Virtue gathered in the past.

The ability to abandon your set ideas depends on how much you have realised your nature and how much you have managed to rid yourself of the ego.

If there is a good store of Virtue, then nothing is impossible.

This is possibly the most important passage of *The Tao Te Ching* and certainly one of the most important teachings of Tai Chi. Once you have found your nature and become one with it, nothing is impossible. The only thing that can limit your life is your lack of imagination. Unfortunately our societies teach otherwise. As soon as possible, children are taught to limit themselves. They are scolded for having too much imagination. The vast majority of adults do not believe that extraordinary things are possible. They do not believe that they can do amazing things or that they can change the world. They do not believe that there is more to life than making a living, reproducing, consuming, and dying.

Tai Chi seeks to destroy the boundaries that society has put upon us and to free the imagination. It seeks to make you as a child once more. Do you wish to write music like Mozart? Do you want to end racial prejudice? Do you wish to free Eastern Europe? You can. Once you have found your nature, once you have become one with yourself, once you have united your will with your Chi, there is nothing that cannot be done. In such a state, you are totally one with the universe and when you move the universe moves with you. All you have to do is have the dream and the will-power.

If nothing is impossible, then there are no limits.

Tai Chi is the seeking of freedom. There is no thought that cannot be thought. There is no dream that cannot be dreamed. There is no person that cannot be loved. Our world is full of cynicism, but you, the Tai Chi person, must dream great dreams. You must shoot for the highest targets and be ready to risk everything. If you can do these things, the Tao will accept you as its own and clutch you to its heart.

One of the most difficult aspects of self-defence, as I have stated before, is the panic that rises when we are confronted by a violent attack. This is especially so when we are small and weak and the attacker is big and strong. In such a situation, we are often filled with despair, and the battle is already lost. When there is no choice and no way to avoid conflict, you must believe in yourself, your destiny, and the power of your Chi. You must will yourself to victory.

The victory will not be to he who is the fastest, or strongest, but rather to he who has the strongest will. You must believe that you will prevail, that with your weakness you can overcome his strength.

The same is true of all the things your nature requires that you do. If your nature demands that you make an attempt to do something, then follow that path. Be unconcerned with whether your actions will be successful, or not. All that is important is the process by which your nature unfolds. This knowledge that your actions are what your nature demands of you will keep you from despair as you face the powerful forces that block your path. The strength and size of those opposing you have no meaning because you are one. You must will yourself through to the fulfilment of your nature.

If a man knows no limits, then he is fit to be a ruler.

If you can be open to all possibilities, if you can harness your will to your Chi energy, if you can unite body, mind, and spirit, if you can tap the deep well of love and compassion that lies at your centre and that is your essence, then you can be the ruler of your own life and the controller of your destiny.

The mother principle of ruling holds good for a long time.

The mother rules her children through love and compassion. These are the forces that the Tai Chi person brings to bear on the world around him in order to fulfil his destiny.

This is called having deep roots and a firm foundation.

Love is the foundation of the Tai Chi life. It is love that makes all things possible. The Tai Chi person must have 'deep roots' in the infinite source of love that lies at his centre.

Verse 60

Ruling the country is like cooking a small fish.

You must be very careful when cooking a small fish or it will fall to pieces. The Tai Chi person must approach everything he does, especially the smallest tasks, with the same carefulness if he wishes to avoid doing more harm than good.

Approach the universe with Tao,
And evil will have no power.
Not that evil is not powerful,

But its power will not be used to harm others.
Not only will it do no harm to others,
But the sage himself will also be protected.
They do not hurt each other,
And the Virtue in each refreshes both.

The Tai Chi person approaches life with Oneness and harmony, rejecting nothing and no one. He realises that there is no such thing as good and evil. There are only harmonious and disharmonious relationships. For example, a piece of lead in the form of a bullet entering a human body does not mean that pieces of lead are evil. It simply means that this is not a harmonious relationship between lead and the human body. When we approach the universe with Oneness, a harmonious relationship is established between ourselves and all that exists. Hence the 'evil' power of all things (that is, disharmonious relationships) will no longer be used to harm others. This also means that the Tai Chi person will be protected from the 'evil' power of things and people. In such a situation, certain qualities in the lead will be allowed to be of benefit to the human being.

One can see that the Tai Chi approach to life is radically different from that of modern society. In our societies, we declare certain things, animals, and people as 'bad', and we seek to destroy them. Such an attitude is responsible for endless warfare, racial violence, religious hatred, and injustice in our legal systems when applied to people. It is responsible for the destruction of the animal world and the environment when applied to animals and things. The Tai Chi approach avoids all of these results by rejecting nothing and no one as evil but, instead, seeking the correct and harmonious relationship between the Tai Chi person and all that exists. In so doing, the Tai Chi person benefits from the unique qualities that exist in all things and people, and all things and people benefit from the nature of the Tai Chi person.

Verse 63

Practice non-action.
Work without doing.

Do only that which your nature requires you to do, and what you do will be without effort or goal. Everything, including the Tai Chi movements, will flow effortlessly from within you when you have learned to 'work without doing'.

Taste the tasteless.

Taste the life of Tao. Find that which is without substance and form. Find the Void and rest within its peace. This is where Tai Chi is leading you.

Magnify the small, increase the few.

Nourish the small beginning you have made toward self-knowledge. Take care of the small things in your life and the big things will take care of themselves.

Reward bitterness with care.

When someone is bitter at you, be very careful. What you do will determine whether the resentment continues and open conflict develops. Use your harmony and peace to root out the bitterness.

See simplicity in the complicated.

Whatever problem in life that you may face, if you can see the cause clearly then you can deal with it. Such a clear vision can only be developed when ambition and attachment have been abandoned, and when you have learned to hold fast to your centre.

Achieve greatness in little things.

Great acts are made up of small deeds. The spinning of the galaxies rests upon the movements of atoms. By controlling the atom, great things can be accomplished. The Tai Chi person learns to understand and control his own movements and by so doing changes the course of the universe.

The sage does not attempt anything very big,
And thus achieves greatness.

The beginning Tai Chi student must not try to grasp the Tai Chi in its entirety from the start. When he takes care to have the correct foot position, the correct balance, and the correct breathing, then all the other aspects of the Tai Chi form will flow of itself. Thus Tai Chi mirrors life. It is best not to attempt anything very big, but to concentrate upon the small things.

Easy promises make for little trust.

The Tai Chi person should speak only when he has something to say. His life must speak for him.

Taking things lightly results in great difficulty.

Everything that occurs in the Tai Chi person's life is of great importance no matter how mundane it might appear. Everything is information that will aid him as he moves in the direction that his nature tells him to. Hence, every second of life is a lesson and everything that exists is his teacher.

Because the sage always confronts difficulties,
He never experiences them.

When the Tai Chi person meets a difficulty, he confronts it. If he reacts spontaneously and immediately to all difficulties as soon he encounters them and while they are still small, his problems will never be insurmountable. This is especially true in relationships with people. As soon as the Tai Chi person perceives anger or resentment, he immediately acts to defuse it with his love and compassion. Thus, conflict is avoided.

Verse 64

Peace is easily maintained.

There must be two persons in order to have conflict, but the Tai Chi person is one with all he meets. When conflict arises, he refuses to participate.

Trouble is easily overcome before it starts.

But trouble is difficult to overcome once it has been allowed to grow to the point of violence. Thus, the Tai Chi person has to make himself very sensitive to the feelings of others so that he can sense trouble before it arises.

The brittle is easily shattered...

That which is not flexible is easily destroyed because it cannot yield and adapt. People with no flexibility of mind, soul, or body are very fragile and easily crushed by adversity. The Tai Chi person must be very gentle with such people.

The small is easily scattered.

If your supply of love and compassion is small, it will be used up very quickly in times of trouble. You must see someone experiencing difficulties before you can really know them. The Tai Chi person's love and compassion for others must be at their strongest in times of trouble.

A tree as great as a man's embrace springs from a small shoot;
A terrace nine storeys high begins with a pile of earth;
A journey of a thousand miles starts under one's feet.

The Tai Chi person is not daunted by the size of any task that his destiny requires of him, or he would not have begun the Tai Chi journey in the first place. He realises that the first step is the most important, as it is the basis upon which all further developments rest. He proceeds by focusing on each step in turn without regard to the end results of his actions. This detachment from success or failure is the result of his having abandoned ambition and goals. He is simply doing that which his nature demands, so why should he care about results? It is the process that is important, not the results.

He who acts defeats his own purpose...

If you act with ambition and attachment, you are moving further and further away from your Oneness with the universe and from Oneness with your true self.

He who grasps loses.

To grasp something, to be attached to something, is to surrender freedom.

The sage does not act, and so is not defeated.

The Tai Chi person has no goal and no ambition, thus he cannot be thwarted. Everything he has, is, and does comes from within himself and cannot be affected by events or the ambitions of people around him. He goes to the Tao depending on nothing and no one but himself.

He does not grasp and therefore does not lose.

Possessing nothing but himself, the Tai Chi person has nothing to lose and thus has no fear of others.

People usually fail when they are on the verge of success.
So give as much care to the end as to the beginning...

There are always people who are great at beginning things but who can never seem to finish what they start. I have had students who have learned 100 of the 108 moves of Tai Chi Chuan and then quit. The Tai Chi person must have the perseverance and willpower to overcome all that keeps him separated from others and from himself. That means that he must maintain his focus from the beginning to the end of his Tai Chi journey. Everything that his nature requires him to do must be done with all of his being all of the time. If this is too much to ask, then the task is not worth doing.

Therefore the sage seeks freedom from desire.
He does not collect precious things.

The Tai Chi person's most precious and only possession is his self-realisation. To possess anything else, he would have to surrender a part of that realisation and a part of that freedom that comes with being one with the Void.

He learns not to hold on to ideas.

In other words, the Tai Chi person must keep an open mind capable of adjusting to an ever-changing world and a never-ending flow of experience.

He brings men back to what they have lost.

By the example of his life and the power of his compassionate love, he helps all with whom he comes into contact to discover their own natures. His very existence reminds people of the Oneness and brotherhood of all things and of all people. This is what we have lost and what keeps us separated in our lives of loneliness.

He helps the ten thousand things find their own nature...

To accept the Tai Chi journey is to accept responsibility for the harmony of the entire universe. Everything that exists must be loved and cherished by he who seeks to be one with the Tao. The person who is loved by another always turns within himself in order to discover what it is that causes such love, and in so doing draws nearer to an understanding of himself and his nature. This is how the Tai Chi person nourishes and helps the world to grow. Love is his only tool and his only protection.

Verse 65

*In the beginning those who knew the Tao did not try
to enlighten others,
But kept them in the dark.*

Those who have achieved Oneness do not try to enlighten others. Everyone must find his own way and what I have experienced will not be of help to you. Each person must experience the Oneness in order to know its reality. People who come to Tai Chi do not come because someone talked them into it or because they thought it was philosophically a good idea. They come because they saw someone doing Tai Chi in a park or on television, and something in the movements touched a place within themselves. And that is the way it should be. I do not like to see advertisements that try to persuade people to learn Tai Chi. A demonstration simply to show the beauty of Tai Chi is fine, but people should only come to Tai Chi if something within them demands it and not because someone has convinced them of the health benefits, etc.

Why is it so hard to rule?
Because people are so clever.

People are clever at manipulating events and other people in an effort to obtain the things they desire. Our whole society is based upon such manipulation, therefore it is very difficult to have a society that is ruled by compassion and concern for others.

Rulers who try to use cleverness
Cheat the country.

A government that manipulates its people will not be of benefit to its citizens and must ultimately fail, since it violates the principles of Tao. But our governments are the product of individual citizens.

We cannot be manipulative in our individual lives and expect to have a community life that is not manipulative. So each individual part of the Tao is responsible for the whole.

Those who rule without cleverness
Are a blessing to the land.

They are a blessing because they allow each person to find his natural state of being rather than the artificial existence that is created by manipulation. Further, they allow an honesty in relationships that is absolutely necessary for the development of Oneness between individuals.

These are the two alternatives.

There are no others. Either you live the life of a manipulator, or you go through life in compassion and unity with others.

Verse 66

Why is the sea king of a hundred streams?
Because it lies below them.
Therefore it is the king of a hundred streams.

All rivers flow to the sea because the sea is lower than all of them. Everything and everyone flows to the Tai Chi person because he accepts the lowest position. He sees himself as the servant of the universe.

If the sage would guide the people, he must serve with humility.

The fully realised Tai Chi person helps others to obtain Oneness by his example; an example based upon humility and compassion. In the Tai Chi school, the further a student goes, the lower his position. For example, if new students are having difficulties, the teacher will take time away from the advanced students in order to spend more time helping the beginners. The further the student goes, the more he is expected to take care of himself. I have purposely missed class to see if the advanced students could carry on without me. As time passes, the advanced student should come to depend upon the teacher less and less until the point is reached where the teacher is no longer needed. Furthermore, behaviour that is allowed for a new student would not be tolerated for advanced students. So the most advanced student is the lowest in the school, just as the most fully developed Tai Chi person is the lowest in life.

If he would lead them, he must follow behind.
In this way when the sage rules, the people will not feel oppressed;
When he stands before them, they will not be harmed.

If you lead by example rather than with power, others will not feel forced, and resentment will not arise. It is the Tai Chi teacher who must set the example of humility for his students both in the

Tai Chi school and in his personal life. The teacher must not live a life filled with luxury and material attachment. Further, he must remember always that his authority in the Tai Chi school results from the Tai Chi tradition and not from his own personal qualities. And, most importantly, he must always keep in mind the fact that he has not succeeded in finding the way to Tao. His teaching is a confession of this. He must be ready to point this out to his students.

One of the most difficult problems for the Tai Chi teacher is those students who come to him expecting to find a guru, someone of vast wisdom who will take them to where they are supposed to be. Such students will be greatly disappointed because the Tai Chi teacher is just another journeyer groping in the dark.

Because he does not compete,
He does not meet competition.

It is impossible to compete with someone who refuses to compete with you. Hence, the Tai Chi person never meets with competition.

Verse 67

This verse represents what the Mother Tao would say to humanity if it spoke to us.

> *Everyone under heaven says that my Tao is great*
> *and beyond compare.*
> *Because it is great, it seems different.*
> *If it were not different, it would have vanished long ago.*

The way of Tai Chi is different from the way of life that people consider to be normal. It is founded upon non-competition, non-violence, non-aggression, compassion, and humility. These are the components of human nature. These are what make us true human beings. These are where harmony and contentment lie. If Tai Chi did not deal with the true nature of things, it would not have survived for so many centuries.

I have three treasures which I hold and keep.
The first is mercy...

The Tai Chi person has three treasures which he carries through life, and the first of these, and the most valuable, is mercy. Only mercy, a feeling of deep compassionate love, can make you one with another. Thus, a feeling of love for all things is essential for the learning of Tai Chi. It is the Tai Chi person's armour and guide. Without this mercy, the movements, the practise, the non-aggression, the flexibility, and so on will mean nothing.

You cannot be one with the universe when you are unable to love others and see no need to love them. One must hear the moaning and weeping of the world and feel some responsibility for ending that suffering: one must have mercy.

the second is economy...

The Tai Chi person must not be wasteful. He must learn from every experience that comes his way and realise that no person or thing is useless. He must speak no wasted words, make no wasted motions, waste no opportunity to discover his nature, and waste no chance to aid others in their journey.

The third is daring not to be ahead of others.

In other words, the Tai Chi person dares to abandon the ego which for most people is the definition of identity. He cuts himself away from the anchor that society has helped him to develop and floats freely upon uncharted seas, letting the current carry him toward his true self. By abandoning the ego, he becomes 'nobody' and, as a result, has no fear of accepting obscurity and the lowest place in life.

From mercy comes courage...

Every parent knows the truth of this statement because of the deep love felt for the child. Parents are willing to accept death in order to protect their child from harm. This is the love that the Tai Chi person must develop for the whole world.

From economy comes generosity...

Because nothing is wasted in the life of the Tai Chi person, he has much left to give to others.

From humility comes leadership.

If you are not seeking reward or recognition, people will trust you.

Nowadays men shun mercy, but try to be brave...

Bravery without compassion is mere ferocity. Such bravery is the trait of a wild beast and is the negation of human nature. No one can deny that soldiers can be extremely brave, but this should be tempered with compassion. Courage is an absolute essential for the Tai Chi way of life but it must be rooted in merciful compassion.

They abandon economy, but try to be generous...

The message of this line is that you cannot give that which you do not have. We all like to think well of ourselves and in times of catastrophe our generosity flows to others in the form of famine relief, accepting refugees, development aid, and so on. But, unless we have centred and rooted ourselves in a deep, compassionate, ever-renewable love for all things, we will soon tire of our efforts. If we have no replenishable source of love to draw upon, our generosity will soon be exhausted. Our own dreams and ambitions will interfere with our efforts. Catastrophes cannot hold our attention for long. We accept refugees until we notice 'too many' in our midst, or until we feel that they threaten our way of life.

I have friends who have a strong love for non-violence, the environment, animal welfare, the poor, etc. They put a great deal of energy into ridding the world of nuclear weapons, cleaning up the environment, and struggling for civil liberties. But as soon as they encounter resistance, they become very hostile and angry with whoever stands in their way. They attack and abuse those who disagree with them. What happened to the love that is supposed to be their motivation?

I once had a friend who used to tell me that guns and armies were evils and that love could overcome all difficulties. He was very proud of himself because he talked a military policeman into giving up his gun. Later, this same friend got a job in a warehouse. After a month of working there, he came to me and asked me if I would show him some self-defence because a man at his workplace was always picking on him. I wondered what happened to his non-violence and love overcoming all difficulties.

The point is that love does overcome all difficulties. The life of Mahatma Gandhi is proof of that. Gandhi lived and died a life of love. He possessed an unending source of love and that love was available to him even as he faced death. My friend did not possess this depth of love. His love came from his intellect and was thus easily exhausted. He could not give that which he did not have.

Tai Chi seeks to help the student establish himself in his Tan Tien, or Chi centre. It is at this point that we are one with the universe and can draw upon all of the energy and love of the Tao. This is the unending source of love that allows the Tai Chi person continuously to give of his love and compassion.

They do not believe in humility, but always try to be first.
This is certain death.

In any form of competition, only one person can be the first. All the others who strive and compete must be losers. This is a terrible waste of resources and energy. And it is 'certain death' because conflict and competition are a sign of separation from others and from one's own nature. If everyone co-operated and harmonised their efforts and talents, all would be winners. Humility is the renunciation of the desire to be first.

Mercy brings victory in battle and strength in defence.

If you are having an argument with someone who feels deep love towards you, it is not easy to remain angry with them. My wife always wins arguments with me because I can always see the love in her eyes. Thus, mercy (compassionate love) brings her victory. And, in defence, love gives strength. A person will find the strength to sacrifice even his life in order to protect those whom he loves.

It is the means by which heaven saves and guards.

This deeply felt love for all things that lies at the centre of us all is the means by which the Tao guides us upon our journey to Oneness. It is the essence of the Tai Chi person's life and his only way of helping the world.

Verse 68

A good soldier is not violent.

It is the soldier who must pay for the conflict between peoples. To be violent only increases the chances that conflict will develop. Thus the Tai Chi person, trained in self-defence, does all that he can to avoid conflict by sustaining within him the qualities of non-violence and non-aggression.

A good fighter is not angry.

When all the ways to avoid conflict have been exhausted and the Tai Chi person must defend himself, he must maintain his tranquillity and compassion during the struggle. Once control of the emotions is lost, it will be impossible to concentrate and the ability to adapt quickly to changing circumstances will vanish. The Tai Chi person only does the bare minimum in order to protect himself and his health. Since he does not lust after victory or fame, self-preservation is all that is required. But to become angry is to lose this restraint.

A good winner is not vengeful.

Winning causes resentment and bitterness in the loser. To be vengeful in victory only increases this resentment which, in turn, increases the chances that the conflict will be renewed at a later time.

A good employer is humble.

To use power, whether financial or physical, to force others to your will, or to lord it over them, causes a feeling of separation and arouses resistance. Power used with humility and for the benefit of all brings forth feelings of love and respect.

This is known as the Virtue of not striving.

Non-competition is essential if one wishes to be one with others and to avoid conflict in life.

Verse 69

There is a saying among soldiers:
I dare not make the first move but would rather play the guest;
I dare not advance an inch but would rather withdraw a foot.

These lines are dealing with the Tai Chi philosophy of yielding in the face of aggression. The Tai Chi person does not meet the aggressor's attack with strength, but rather he withdraws so the opponent has nothing to stop his momentum. His momentum makes him lose his balance as he finds no resistance, and it is then the Tai Chi person strikes. There are no attacks in Tai Chi.

This is called marching without appearing to move,
Rolling up your sleeves without showing your arm...

The Tai Chi person is always prepared for self-defence while never making a show of his art. The demonstration of skill in the martial arts can cause fear in others or it can arouse envy and invite attack by those who wish to see if they are better than you.

Capturing the enemy without attacking...

The aggressor's underestimation of your ability will allow your weakness to overcome his strength.

Being armed without weapons.

If you know absolutely nothing about self-defence and you are attacked by someone, your only recourse is to use a weapon. The less you know, the more violent you have to be. Being prepared and able to use your body and flexibility makes weapons and violence unnecessary.

There is no greater catastrophe than
underestimating the enemy.

The Tai Chi person wishes this catastrophe to be with his attacker, and not with himself.

Therefore when the battle is joined,
The underdog will win.

When the attack against you is made, it will come as a tremendous surprise to the aggressor that he cannot overcome you who seem so weak and incapable.

Verse 70

This verse is again the Mother Tao talking to humanity.

My words are easy to understand and easy to perform,
Yet no man under heaven knows them or practises them.

The ways of the Tao are natural and flow without effort. To know and understand them, we need only look within ourselves. But humanity has fallen away from the Oneness. We are separated not only from the universe, but from our own nature. We have surrendered our intuitive knowledge to a complete worship of the rational mind and to its creation, the ego, which operates on the basis of attachment to desires.

My words have ancient beginnings.

From the beginning of creation, non-violence, compassion, non-aggression, and non-competition have always been the essence of the Tao.

My actions are disciplined.

The Tao flows spontaneously, but not chaotically. Its movements follow certain principles. Tai Chi teaches these principles and helps the student to learn to move with them.

Because men do not understand, they have no knowledge of me.

In our society, people have no respect for nature and no respect for individual uniqueness. Our society is totally consumed by the desire for possession and attainment. Therefore, it is almost impossible for us to see the Oneness that flows through all people and things. Because of this, the Tao and its harmony are unknown to us.

Those that know me are few;
Those that abuse me are honoured.
Therefore the sage wears rough clothing
and holds the jewel in his heart.

In our society, those who violate nature and abuse man's humanity in the name of progress are rewarded. Those who live in humility without ambition are scorned. The Tai Chi person mourns the lost harmony of the universe and all the pain and destruction that are the result of this loss. He holds to the 'jewel', his deep love and compassion for all that is, as he moves through life towards himself and his destiny.

Verse 72

When men lack a sense of awe, there will be disaster.

When a man sees an extremely beautiful woman, it can be awe-inspiring. The awestruck simply stares, unable to believe such beauty. The sun can be awesome as it rises over the mountains. The experience of it overwhelms you. The harmony of the universe, the perfection, the timing, whether of the spinning of the galaxies, or the flow of blood in the human body, or the activity of the brain, or the birth of a child; it is all awesome. These things cause awe because they are complete. Nothing can be added or taken away without ruining the perfection.

When we lose the ability to feel awe in the face of beauty and perfection, when nature becomes plastic to us, just something to use and then throw away, disaster must result. When we are no longer awed by the majesty of the mountains, but see them simply as sources of ore or ski resorts, when we no longer see the overwhelming beauty of the forest but only a place to dump our rubbish, we will have lost the essence of life.

We are so used to being entertained that everything in our world can seem dull and boring. We are so concerned with the fulfilment of our own desires that there is no place we fear to tread and no situation in which we are loath to interfere. That is why our lives are so empty.

Do not intrude in their homes.
Do not harass them at work.

The Tai Chi person must accept people as they are. In his sensitivity, he respects the unique nature of each individual and does not judge his journey through life. I had a friend once who converted to Buddhism. I never asked him why he did it. That was something between him and his god. Who am I to step between these two? It is too awesome a relationship for me to interfere.

Therefore the sage knows himself but makes no show...

The Tai Chi journey moves the student toward self-knowledge: a clear insight into who and what he is. But the Tai Chi person wishes to pass through life as unnoticed as possible in order that his life of harmony remains undisturbed.

Has self-respect but is not arrogant...

He knows his abilities and his weaknesses, but his self-respect does not mean that he loses respect for others.

He lets go of that and chooses this.

He lets go of everything that would take him outside of himself and holds to his centre.

Verse 73

A brave and passionate man will kill or be killed.
A brave and calm man will always preserve life.

Bravery in the face of danger is an essential quality for the Tai Chi person. But there is a difference between someone who is brave and at peace with himself and someone who is brave but lost in his passions, like the soldier in wartime. Such a soldier can demonstrate tremendous courage. The brave and calm man will demonstrate the same amount of courage in trying to preserve life. He has the courage to face the attacker while striving not to harm him. In some of the martial arts, the philosophy is to strike as hard and as quickly as possible in order to do the utmost damage. Such a philosophy is completely contradictory to the philosophy of Tai Chi.

In Tai Chi, the idea is to avoid giving pain. According to an ancient story, a teacher and his pupil were walking through the jungle and saw a wild boar. In the distance, a lion roared. The wild boar looked up, saw the lion coming and ran away. The student asked the teacher why the wild boar did not stay to fight, since he had large tusks with which to kill the lion. The teacher replied that the boar could have stayed to fight and saved his life by killing the lion, but, by running away, the boar saved two lives.

Of these two, which is good and which is harmful?

Bravery will always be a necessity for human development, but it must be allied to self-awareness and a love for all things.

The Tao of heaven does not strive, and yet it overcomes.

The Tao makes no effort to do anything. It follows its own nature, flowing wherever its principles take it and, in so doing, overcomes everything in its path, setting the pattern for the Tai Chi life.

It does not speak, and yet it is answered.

Not seeking anything, it has all that it needs. It does not talk and yet the heart of the Tai Chi person responds to it.

It seems at ease, and yet it follows a plan.

Though the Tao moves spontaneously, there are certain principles that it always follows. This is also true of the Tai Chi person. He moves spontaneously, but his life is ruled by the principles of non-violence, non-aggression, and compassion.

Heaven's net casts wide.
Though its meshes are coarse, nothing slips through.

The Tao encompasses everything. Though there is a great amount of room for diversity and uniqueness, everything is a part of the same Oneness.

Verse 76

A man is born gentle and weak.
At his death he is hard and stiff.
Green plants are tender and filled with sap.
At their death they are withered and dry.
Therefore the stiff and unbending is the disciple of death.
The gentle and yielding is the disciple of life.

Softness and flexibility are signs of life. Hardness and stiffness are signs of death. The live branch of a tree is too yielding to be broken but the dead limb lying on the ground is stiff and snaps easily. If your body is inflexible, it is a sign of approaching death. You can tell how old someone is by how far he can bend his back. No matter what your age, if your back is still flexible, you are young. Thus, Tai Chi concentrates on the joints in order to keep them flexible and youthful. My style of Tai Chi is very extended and requires a great amount of flexibility. I have seen many elderly people come to the school, observe our form and decide that they could never do such movements. But of those who stayed, there were none who did not succeed in becoming flexible enough to do the form. It does not matter how old or inflexible the student is, with patience the lost flexibility of youth can be recaptured.

Thus an army without flexibility never wins a battle.

The Tai Chi person who cannot adapt to every situation will not be able to overcome the difficulties he meets in life.

A tree that is unbending is easily broken.

People who have no flexibility can be damaged more easily, and are more likely to lose their freedom, than those who are able to bend.

The hard and strong will fall.
The soft and weak will overcome.

Those who go through life depending upon hardness and strength must fall because there is always someone harder and stronger. But those who face life with the softness and weakness of love and compassion become one with the universe and can overcome all obstacles in their path.

Verse 77

The Tao of heaven is like the bending of a bow.
The high is lowered, and the low is raised.
If the string is too long, it is shortened.
If there is not enough, it is made longer.

Those who seek to be high with fame and money are violating the principles of the Tao and will never find Oneness, peace, and harmony. Thus, the high are lowered. Those who live a life of humility and who are moving towards Oneness with all things will succeed because the universe is with them. Thus they achieve the highest pinnacle of human existence.

The Tao of heaven is to take from those who have too much and
give to those who do not have enough.
Man's way is different.
He takes from those who do not have enough to give to those who
already have too much.

The way of the Tao is the way of love. It is human nature for those who have to give to the needy. If this desire to share is missing, humanity itself is missing. The trait of sharing and caring for others is evident in primitive tribal communities and rural societies but becomes lost in large urban societies where people feel separated and alienated from others. Our societies are designed so that the people on the bottom carry the heaviest load and receive the least reward. There is a great imbalance between the rich and the poor and this imbalance is the cause of most of our social problems. It is an imbalance created by human greed and desire that overcomes a natural love of humanity.

What man has more than enough and gives it to the world?
Only the man of Tao.

As long as you can take care of your bodily needs, everything else in your life is extra. The extra is what you share with the world. In the philosophy of Tai Chi there is nothing wrong with the idea of being rich if wealth comes as a natural result of your work and is not something that is striven after. Wealth is only harmful when it is hoarded and used for individual gratification. The wealthy person should only serve as a conduit through whose hands wealth flows toward those in need. The natural resources of the earth are limited, and some people, for whatever reason, cannot receive their share. If you have more than you need, you are taking from these people and it is up to you to see that they receive their part. Your wealth will not be resented if it is used to help the world to find harmony and peace.

Further, there is one thing the Tai Chi person possesses in tremendous abundance: love for others. This abundance is available to all whom he meets. This is the true wealth of the Tai Chi person.

Verse 78

Under heaven nothing is more soft and yielding than water.
Yet for attacking the solid and strong, nothing is better;
It has no equal.

As stated earlier, water is one of the most important symbols of Taoist thinking and Tai Chi. It is soft and yielding, and yet it overcomes the strength of the rock in its path. In Tai Chi, we say, 'stand like a mountain, flow like a river'. The river makes the land fertile and gives of itself to all that exists. The ability of water to change, to fit any shape, allows it to overcome anything in its path.

Water has no goal. The river moves towards the ocean simply because that is its nature. It does not seek the ocean and it makes no effort to reach it. The river is merely itself and it flows to the ocean because that is what rivers do.

The Tai Chi person uses water as an example for his own life. He trains to become adaptable so that he can adjust to every situation. He becomes soft and yielding so that he can overcome obstacles in his path. He does not judge others, but offers his nature to all whom he meets, rejecting no one. His compassion is there for the saint as well as for the murderer. And he has no ambition, nor any goal. He moves towards Oneness because that is his nature. Though he helps the universe find harmony, he seeks no fame or reward.

The weak can overcome the strong;
The supple can overcome the stiff.

It is our flexibility that helps us to overcome those who are inflexible when we are forced to use Tai Chi self-defence. Inflexible people are unable to manoeuvre and adjust to new situations. Thus, their responses are limited.

Under heaven everyone knows this,
Yet no one puts it into practise.

Our whole society is based on the use of strength and force. However, if you go through life using strength and force, someday you must meet someone who is stronger. Thus, strength and force must ultimately fail.

Therefore the sage says:
He who takes upon himself the humiliation of the people is fit to
rule them.
He who takes upon himself the country's disasters deserves to be
king of the universe.

This understanding is sadly lacking in our politicians. Whenever there is a disaster, the people in the government seek to shift the blame. The disaster was some other department's fault or it was caused by some other country. People in government want power, but seek to avoid responsibility. What is responsibility? Responsibility and duty are what define an adult human being. We are responsible for the harmony of the universe because it is humanity that has destroyed it. The universe will never reach a state of harmony without you finding harmony within your own life first. Thus, the universe depends upon you to do that which is required of you. It is the Tai Chi person who accepts this responsibility.

Verse 79

After a bitter quarrel, some resentment must remain.
What can one do about it?

There is really nothing that one can do about it. The history of the world is a history of such resentment. Such resentment comes from having been exploited, or having been humiliated, or having been conquered, and it can last for centuries. Therefore, the Tai Chi person does his utmost to avoid conflict and the manipulation of others. If the Tai Chi person must use Tai Chi to defend himself, it is a sign that he has failed in his journey. The whole point of Tai Chi is to become one with others. The use of self-defence shows that the Tai Chi person has lost his way.

Therefore the sage keeps his half of the bargain
But does not exact his due.
A man of Virtue performs his part,
But a man without Virtue requires others to fulfil their obligations.

In any kind of bargain, do that which is required of you, but expect no one else to do the same. If you have no expectations from other people, you will never be disappointed, and therefore will never have cause for animosity, conflict, and resentment. People desire to be honest and fair but the ego, with its ambition and greed, interferes with this natural tendency. The failure of others should not give rise to anger but, rather, to compassion.

Verse 81

Truthful words are not beautiful.
Beautiful words are not truthful.

Many people use beautiful words to manipulate others. Politicians specialise in this ability. The Tai Chi person must learn to go beyond words and experience the heart of others.

Good men do not argue.
Those who argue are not good.

People who have reached Oneness with all things and who have found peace and harmony within themselves have no need to argue. Argument is a sign of failure to erase separation.

Those who know are not learned.
The learned do not know.

Those who understand how to live with the world around them do not necessarily have formal educations. They may not be learned in the intellectual discipline of commanding facts in order to manipulate objects and people. Those who can merely command facts do not understand what true knowledge is. True knowledge is the understanding of the Oneness of all life.

The sage never tries to store things up.

This moment is the most important moment of your life. Take care of this moment and the future will take care of itself.

The more he does for others, the more he has.
The more he gives to others, the greater his abundance.

The more I help you towards realisation of your own nature, the closer I move towards realisation of my own. The closer that you come to Oneness with all things, the closer I come to such Oneness.

The Tao of heaven is pointed but does no harm.
The Tao of the sage is work without effort.

The way of the universe, the way of all life, operates for the benefit of all creatures. In order to be in harmony with this way, the Tai Chi person discovers his own nature and follows it to his destiny.

4
The Tai Chi Teacher

No one can know with the mind what Tai Chi and the Tao are. These are things which cannot be grasped with the mind. One can only stand in awe of them. The Tai Chi journey is thus a journey without signposts or guides. This means that the traveller is completely on his own. There is no guru, guide, or authority that can say, 'This is the way'. Each of us must find our own nature and flow with it where it leads us. Just as the river finds the ocean because its nature takes it there, the Tai Chi person needs no guide or map to take him to the harmony and peace of the Tao: his nature will take him there. Tai Chi is simply a means to help the traveller find and become one with his nature. Whither that nature takes the student, no one can say. None other can know your journey.

The Tai Chi teacher is merely someone who has learned a little through his own Tai Chi experience. He does not know the way to Oneness. If he did, he would no longer be teaching but would have arrived at Oneness and disappeared into the Void. Hence the saying, 'He who speaks does not know. He who knows does not speak.'

The task of the Tai Chi student is to find a teacher who, he trusts, has experienced Tai Chi in its reality and who is moving towards a life of harmony. When the student feels that he has found such a teacher, he learns as much as he can from him. At some point, the student realises that he can learn no more from this teacher. This does not mean that the teacher has nothing more to teach, but that this particular student has nothing more to learn from this teacher for reasons that cannot be explained. It is something that both the student and the teacher should feel. It is time then for the student to seek out another teacher who can take the student a little further. This process continues as long as the student remains on his journey.

The teacher also is on a journey. There can be no such thing as a professional Tai Chi teacher. Teaching is but a stage in the Tai Chi person's journey. The traveller should continuously alternate between the roles of teacher and student until he reaches the point where he has obtained Oneness with himself and the universe and disappears into the Void. When I hear of Tai Chi teachers who are ninety years old and who have been teaching for sixty or seventy years, I wonder how their journey went so wrong. Why have they not found the Tao?

I grew up in Texas in a cowboy family and I was a cowboy for several years there and in New Mexico. There has never been anything that I have ever enjoyed as much as being a cowboy, but I knew that there was something missing in my life that would never be fulfiled while I remained in that job. Thus, I began the Tai Chi journey and eventually became a teacher. When I have obtained Oneness with myself and the universe, I will go back to being a cowboy and 'disappear' from the world of Tai Chi, to teach no more, to study no more, but simply to be. As the old Zen poem says:

Before enlightenment, chopping wood, carrying water.
After enlightenment, chopping wood, carrying water.

And that is the whole message of Tai Chi; it does not matter what you do, but that you do it with awareness and Oneness.

The Tai Chi school is a ship that sails towards the Tao upon uncharted seas. The teacher is the captain of the ship. He is a captain who does not know the way, but he can handle a ship and he has a good feeling for the sea. He guides his ship by relying upon his own intuition and his past experience of the journey. He has no chart or guide. Sometimes he will continue upon his course despite the fact that people are telling him that it is the wrong way. But these people do not know it is the wrong way, they only believe it is. How could they know since they have never been to the Tao? If they had, they would not be giving advice. When the teacher makes a decision and finds that it was indeed not the way, he will be ridiculed by those who told him so in the beginning. But the difference is that the teacher now knows that it is not the way because he went there. The ones who did not make the journey only believe it is not the way.

In other words, the Tai Chi teacher is experimenting with life. Every second of his life, he stands at a crossroads with no sign to point the way. Everything he does is a risk, a gamble. Sometimes he may seem gentle and kind and, at others, harsh and dictatorial. Sometimes he may seem morally reprehensible and at other times a saint. Such swings of direction may be confusing to the student if the student does not understand the experimentation the teacher must engage in if he is to find the way. The student should only stay with his teacher as long as he has trust that his teacher is indeed trying to find the Tao. If the student loses that trust, then he should leave the school and find another teacher. If the teacher has the answer to every question and is always the same, either he has found Oneness and should no longer be teaching, or he is not really on the Tai Chi journey.

The school, our ship, exists for those students who are travelling toward the Tao. In a school of 100 students, perhaps there will be two or three such students. Others will be there for various reasons: health, fascination with things oriental, the grace and beauty of the moves, etc. These students are welcome because they help in the financial maintenance of the school and because Tai Chi will help them, but the school exists for those two or three who are travelling toward the Tao. I have had students who did not want to wear traditional black, did not like incense, did not want to learn certain Tai Chi disciplines, did not want to hear the philosophy, or wanted to learn more quickly. Such students must realise that the school will not change and that they must adjust to it or leave. The school is not a recreation centre where you come on Thursday night to meet the girls, or because there is nothing good on television that evening. Students are welcome to stay as long as they adapt to the school and do not expect the school to adapt to them.

Teachers who adapt their school in order to keep a large number of students lose the essence of their discipline. I once entered a judo school and saw an aikido class practising to blaring rock music. Beer was sold between classes. Such a school has ceased to be 'a place of the way' and has become an amusement centre.

The student must see that the Tai Chi teacher is not just concerned with the Tai Chi movements, the flow of Chi, meditational stances, etc., but also understands the philosophy and the way of life that are the background of the discipline. For example, there are dance teachers who teach Tai Chi and who can perform beautiful movements, but that is all that their movements are: a performance. They have no idea what Tai Chi is but see it as simply another dance.

There are teachers who have a profound knowledge of how to raise and use the Chi energy, who know powerful meditations, and who can do amazing things with Chi Gung (exercises to raise the Chi energy), but who never mention the need for their students to ground their lives in compassion and mercy.

Another type of teacher to be avoided is the teacher who has won trophies in competitions and has instituted rankings and coloured belts as signs of progress. Such a teacher has never grasped the basic principle of non-competition that is at the heart of Tai Chi. With such a teacher, Tai Chi becomes a sport.

Self-advertisement is another sign that a teacher has failed to grasp the principles of Tai Chi. There are Tai Chi teachers who are always getting articles about themselves in the newspapers and giving interviews on television. Tai Chi is the way of humility. We do not advertise ourselves. A simple notice in the paper that a class is beginning is enough. If the teacher is a true Tai Chi teacher offering authentic Tai Chi, he will need no advertisement of himself or of his skills. He will be sought out by those who are truly seeking.

Finally, it must be remembered that the Tai Chi teacher is the Earth Father. Just as the father must provide his children with every chance for the best education possible, the Tai Chi teacher must provide his students with every chance for the fullest development of their nature. The teacher must provide a place where the student can come to practise alone in order to get to know his own Chi and to feel his own uniqueness. He must provide a class so that the student can learn to become one with a group of people by harmonising his Chi with theirs. He must keep expanding the horizons of what is possible. In other words, his whole life must be dedicated to the welfare of his students as long as he assumes the role of a teacher. In my own case, all my revenue including the proceeds from this book goes towards the buying of land and the founding of a Tai Chi Centre in the mountains where students can come for varying periods of time in order to experiment with Tai Chi living.

What all of the above is trying to point out is that it is not easy to find a true Tai Chi teacher. One of the purposes of this book is to give the student an idea of what Tai Chi is so that he will know when he has found such a teacher. The greater the teacher is, the harder he will be to find.

5
Conclusion

I am a Tai Chi journeyer. I do not know where I am going for I have never been there. I do not know the way because I have never met anyone who can tell me how to get there. Thus, the words of this book are meaningless. They are only words that try to express feelings. But, like all words, they cannot carry truth. My words can simply hint at a universe where there are no limits and where everything is possible. It is a universe filled with an ever-surging ocean of love whose whirlpools, tides, and streams touch upon all that is. To enter this ocean is to travel the vast empty spaces of the soul, dependent upon no one but yourself. I can be forgotten because I am not important. This book can be forgotten because it is unimportant. But if this book has given you the merest glimpse of the fantastic voyage that is Tai Chi, then hold that glimpse as a precious jewel deep in your heart and it will keep you warm when you encounter the cold hard places that you meet in life as you make your own journey to the Mother Tao, which, in the end, is yourself.